NOURISHED

by

DIVERSITY

Creating A Legacy of Inclusion and Community For Your Organization to Shine

LEAD YOUR DESIGN

— BY JALEH ZANDIEH —

These stories are based on actual events.

Even the ones that seem too good to be true...
they actually happened.

Don't you love real stories based on genuine people
doing really cool things?

The first dedication goes to you, dear Reader.

_This book is dedicated to the continuous development of your
innate talents, strengths, and qualities that enable you to feel more
empowered, appreciated, and capable of joyful service to humanity.
May these stories activate the incredible elements within you that
make you feel expansive, hopeful, and truly alive.
May you see more of the possibilities that reside within you,
and from that state of steadiness and readiness,
feel inspired to see the potential in others.
May you enjoy the stories and feel reminded that there are lots
of good people in the world, and the more they feel
their capacities to do good grow stronger, the greater
the whole of humanity can improve._

_Second, this book is dedicated to those in the world who are actively
seeking a path of service that comes from a place of joy and kindness
towards their fellow human beings. May your path of service reveal
itself with confirmations that act as guideposts so you continue to
honor yourself as you develop your capacity to say and do things that
bring more light to your life - and to the lives of others._

_Third, to my "A-Team" who continuously encourage me, support me,
and believe in me… even when I don't see what they see.
Theirs are the voices that activate my courage to speak and express
myself, to choose to care rather than become jaded,
and to walk my path of service._

*Thank you for believing in me until I could train my belief
muscles and trust myself enough to take the next step.
Thank you for not requiring proof of success until your care,
love, and true friendship could reach me.*

*Thank you for creating a space for me to belong,
regardless of who or what I represent, what my name is, where I was
born, who raised me, and how I look and move through the world.*

*Thank you for the blessing of you in my life.
Thank you for being the calm during the storms;
for being the warmth when I was in a wave of sadness;
for being the confetti of joyful celebration when I crossed a finish line;
for being the lighthouse showing me where
I was and where I was headed;
for being the wisdom when I was overwhelmed and under-prepared;
for being the best hugs to embrace all of me;
for being the trustworthy beacon during layers of doubts and fears;
for being a home of peace when my heart needed
the nourishment of kindness;
for being the voice that activates my curiosity
to keep learning and growing;
for being a reminder that I can be at home in many places in the
world because of our genuine bonds of love.*

*I wouldn't be me if you weren't you…
So thank you for being you.
My world - our entire world - is better because you're part of it.*

NOURISHED BY DIVERSITY

By Jaleh Zandieh

Edited and published by:

The Boss Books/Libri d'Impresa Publishing

Denise Cumella Srl

via Togliatti 5D

200085 Locate di Triulzi (MI), Italy

www.thebossbooks.com

ISBN 9791281385016

CONTENTS

9 SERVICE-DRIVEN LEADERSHIP STYLES IN THIS FRAMEWORK

We cannot wait all of our lives with the hope
of reaching a state of inner perfection
before we act.
Even the smallest of flames gives
warmth and light.
In fact, the flame cannot help
but to give warmth.
Motivation to serve comes from within,
and one arises to render service
not out of begrudging sense of duty
but because service is a natural state of being.

Dr. Farzam Arbab

WELCOME, DEAR READER

Nourished By Diversity is a book that highlights 20 years of original research that focuses on people from around the world who lead their lives with a core value of service - and how they're able to contribute to the well-being of people and their communities within their sphere of influence.

My desire is to lay out this framework to you to experience the patterns that came from the work I've done over the last two decades. It's designed to offer a process for you to take notice of the qualities you possess that bring more goodness into the world and to fall more in love with these parts of yourself.

Two of the main themes that run through the course of this book are: the valuable role that diversity plays in creating a community and culture that thrives; and how cross-sections of diversity help people serve others in a more impactful and more joyful way.

Instead of being an obstacle to true connection, community, and unity, what if diversity was meant to be a nourishing, vibrant, helpful element that unlocks the doors to more health, well-being, innovation, capacity-building, and a legacy that makes the next generations more capable of living fulfilling, happy lives?

Diversity has always been a part of life, for which I am eternally grateful. If my life was a book, the first page of the first chapter — my birth certificate — would represent diversity. Having a mother and father who represent different nationalities, cultures, backgrounds, languages, and traditions, my life has always found a way to include a blend, a mix, an "and". My favorite word in any language I've ever learned is a three-letter word, simple yet profound, that erases the notion of separate. Instead, this word creates a sense of belonging, in which two things can be bridged, knit, or combined together. It's a word that doesn't erase differences, but rather carves a space where multiple things can exist harmoniously. This word is "and". I told you it was a simple word, but it changed my life.

One of the people who made a profound impact on my life was my 92-year-old mentor when I was living in China. He noticed that I would often phrase questions in terms of "this or that" and that I constantly used "or" in my language. Then, one day he gave me a challenge to replace "or" with "a better word", and that I should meditate on what that "better word" is. He often challenged the way I thought about things that limited me or caused more pain, and he gave me a clue for this particular challenge.

"*Think about your name. Say it. Write it. Return to your name.*" I had a feeling that his words would make sense later, but in the moment, I got more confused and started digging deep into what my name meant in Mandarin and what it means in its original language of Persian. After riding my bike around the town and thinking about his advice, lightning struck, and my mind had a thought I never had before.

"My last name is Zandieh… 'and' is in my name!"

So excited that I had figured out the riddle, I rode my bike back to his office with a bag of sweet oranges to share with him. They were one of his favorite fruits.

When I opened the door and saw him standing with a hot cup of green tea, he smiled at me, as though he already knew I had found the answer to his challenge.

What he said to me still brings a big smile to my face,
"Welcome to the Land of And."

That's the translation of what he spoke in that bright moment of my fresh insight. That was the day I decided that my favorite word was 'and'.

So, I invite you, dear Reader, and welcome you to the "Land of And".

This book highlights the often much-overlooked benefits of having more diversity — more "and" — in our lives.

To do this, we'll focus on exploring 3 of the 9 Service-Driven Leadership Styles in this framework. These chapters will spotlight real-life heroes who made a significant impact in my life by embodying the qualities of their respective Leadership Style. These heroes also represent many types of diversity, including race, gender, generation, nationality, ethnicity, language, and heritage.

I'm grateful and appreciate everything that makes them who they are: internal and external, visible and invisible. It's a gift to be able to see them, notice them, value them, cherish them, and honor them — for all of those distinctive qualities create the one-of-a-kind tapestry that makes us each a full human being.

Each chapter will also provide you the opportunity to appreciate these qualities in yourself.

Exploring our own unique vantage points and practicing ways to express our talents are powerful ways to train our "leadership muscles". This is particularly effective when we adopt a posture of learning to also recognize the variety of talents and contributions that others can offer.

With a united vision and shared goals, we often benefit from collaborating with people who have perspectives, skills, expertise, and experiences different from our own. This is because we cover each other's "blind spots" or areas of less awareness.

The following Leadership Styles — although highly distinct from each other — make a strong, vibrant, effective team and community. They are not meant to be competitive with each other. On the contrary, the research shows that they can become complementary because their qualities and strengths each move the needle of progress forward.

This model of leadership also supports more sustainability by helping to prevent overwhelming stress, exhaustion, and burnout due to few people having the weight of the world on their shoulders. A thriving, united, effective team and culture helps any project or goal become more possible and long-lasting.

The power comes from all of the rich diversity that the community members represent and express.

My hope is for this book to help tune your own instrument and play in key with the way you're designed — to make beautiful music and then experience the joy of playing in harmony with others.

ALLOW ME TO INTRODUCE MYSELF

For as long as I can remember, I have been a person who has a deep curiosity to understand things that seemed important and impacted people. Even if the mystery seemed beyond my current capacity to figure out, I wanted to ask the questions that could lead to even small realizations.

I didn't like it when adults would brush off my questions with phrases like:
"Because that's how it is," or "That's the way it's always been," or "You're still young and don't have to worry about it... it doesn't concern you yet."

I couldn't understand how people wouldn't try to figure out the answers to questions that could lead to more clarity and help complex things make sense.

My sincere desire to connect the dots and discover how things affect each other has been part of how I see the world, even as an inquisitive 4-year-old new big sister of my little brother.

This search for truth and discovery of wonder continued throughout my life — in each decade — and has helped each part of my life to this day. It is particularly helpful with my clients who greatly value getting more clarity so that they can lead their companies and organizations with as much awareness and understanding as possible.

They were actually the ones representing great forces of encouragement to publish my work and write about my framework so that it could help more people.

When I started writing this book, I wanted it to provide lots of value, clarity, meaningful information, and helpful patterns that I've learned from working with leaders from around the world.

My goal was for the book to share the information that I found to be exceptionally valuable, as well as tell stories from real experiences that help to bring the information to life through connecting with fellow humans that we can relate to.

It was also important to me to create a book that — in addition to providing practical steps — also feels like a letter of gratitude to the people who guided me every step of the way. These individuals foster a warmth, a light, and a treasure chest of qualities that I wish everyone in the world to experience.

It's deeply gratifying to help people learn about this framework and implement the content that highlights the importance of diversity in service-driven leadership. Wonderful ripple effects began taking off and my clients and communities were able to connect service with what enables them to feel in greater alignment with their "gems of inestimable value".

This supports an ecosystem that's dedicated to higher levels of integrity, impact and joy.

When I was thinking what to name this book that has the tall order of summarizing the foundational beliefs, people, stories, experiences, learnings, and framework that has informed my entire professional path — and often my personal life — I knew I had to include one word. This word is the essence of my life. It's a metaphor for my entire story. This word is **diversity**.

If my life was a book, this word would describe the first page. If my life was a movie, this word would have to be in the opening credits. It describes why my first and last name is Persian, and my middle name, Martha, is used in many languages and cultures yet has its original roots in Aramaic, meaning "lady".

It describes the atmosphere of every holiday, celebration, and special event that I experienced growing up. It describes why I felt at home growing up in Harrisburg, Pennsylvania in the United States, yet also felt at home when I lived in China, Sweden, and Portugal.

Diversity describes why I had my first passport stamp at the mature age of two months.
My first passport photo had the arms of my mother cradling my head and supporting my small frame, which would have probably been funny for the personnel at Customs.

The word diversity describes how my father found his second home and "adopted" family in the United States at the young age of 16.

This word is a reflection of how my birthday parties and wedding were described by guests as a "mini version of a United Nations". (Sidenote: I actually got to participate at a UN event many years later when I served as a guest presenter.)

"Nourished by Diversity" also highlights the patterns of my research and people who inspire me every day. It also tells true-life stories of 3 heroic people in my life who each embody one of the Leadership Styles covered in this book that have a common foundational value of service to humanity.

I look forward to continuing to share this framework with people and organizations, groups and teams, companies and countries who want to pursue purposeful service that is an extension and expression of their values, vision, and voices.

Together, we can achieve remarkable, extraordinary things that make the world a healthier, safer, more thriving place for everyone.

Thank you for allowing me to share my vision and experiences with you. May they serve you well and contribute to your highest good.

1

THE EARLY DAYS: HOW DIVERSITY BEGAN NOURISHING MY LIFE

Regard man as a mine rich in gems
of inestimable value.
Education can, alone,
cause it to reveal its treasures,
and enable mankind to benefit therefrom.
Bahá'u'lláh

I grew up playing the flute and the tenor and alto saxophones, which are all woodwind instruments, but they have a variety of differences too. Neither instrument is better than the others. They each provide a distinctive sound, quality of tone, and style of notes that make the music come to life.

A big thank you to Mr. Miles and Mr. Corey for believing in me, encouraging me, and teaching me these three incredible instruments. You both allowed me to experience the soaring happiness of making music with a group of musicians and learn about ourselves in creative, disciplined, fun ways. You both helped me receive the sweet blessings of learning in a diverse community where the goal was excellence and there was always room to grow.

Learning about music helped me learn about people and the many complexities that each person brings.

Every instrument is primed to play in tune with itself, but this requires skill and training. Every instrument is also designed to play in tune with other instruments that are similar and different than itself — creating layers of beautiful melodies and harmonies — and this also requires skill, practice, and training.

For example, the saxophone has a golden color, is larger and heavier, requires a neck strap to hold most of the weight so your arms don't get tired while playing, it sits perpendicular to the ground, requires a wooden reed on the mouthpiece to play, has a blend of curves, projects its sound louder, and creates a rich, soulful sound that always reminds me of jazz.

On the other hand, the flute's appearance is naturally lighter, has a silver color, has a straight design and has no curves. It is played while being held horizontally, so it's parallel to the floor.
There is no reed necessary to play the flute. Its tone tends to be softer and plays notes of higher octaves.

Yet, they have something in common that's invisible and essential... the key they're designed to play in.

For example, the alto saxophone is an E-flat instrument, just like the baritone saxophone.
The tenor saxophone is a B-flat instrument, which is the same as a trumpet and clarinet.
The flute is a C instrument, like the piano, oboe, and violin — which all look and sound quite different.

As I continued to play music during my years as a student, I realized how much some instruments had in common based on their appearance, yet they were designed to play and sound differently. Meanwhile, they actually had some important things in common with instruments that looked quite different.

I found it fascinating how certain instruments can make such beautiful melodies together — despite all the layers of diversity — and their differences don't form obstacles to creating musical masterpieces because they find ways to utilize their distinctive qualities and harmonize them together.

Much like musical instruments, people are a composite of layers of distinctive qualities — both external and internal.

People can represent a range of observable qualities, such as: heritage, cultures, languages, geographic places, nationalities, sizes, shapes, colors, hues, strengths, capacities, abilities, ages, generations, and many others.

People also represent internal diversity that's not as easily observable, such as: temperament, vantage points, perspectives, dreams, values, cares, needs, loves, fears, joys, doubts, stress points, celebrations, longing, regrets, priorities, understanding, awareness, experiences, and many others.

Nourished by Diversity will begin exploring a process for cultivating a thriving community and culture that consistently appreciates, values, and benefits from 9 distinctive vantage points.

Each of these vantage points — or Leadership Lenses — help any organization, company, or business create a legacy of inclusion and service to the well-being of humanity.

Imagine what would be possible if more people could learn how to play their unique instruments — staying in tune as often as possible — while also learning how to play with other instruments.

What if only similar instruments are the only ones trying to play a symphony together?

How much richness of sound would be left missing?

What if a blend of diverse instruments could come together — staying in tune with themselves throughout the process — and created something so beautiful that it would change the way people felt when they listened to their collective expression?

This is one way to think about the power of diversity having a role to build bridges, meaningful connections, conscious communities, and be part of the nuanced solutions that answer humanity's current challenges.

We'll explore the essential leadership "nutrients" that allow people to sustain their spark for service without burning out from the work that lights them up.

One of the important leadership nutrients that supports every great service-driven leader is a thriving culture of diversity. This book will highlight real-life heroes of different backgrounds who serve as Ambassadors of their respective Leadership Style, and how they're able to lead their lives with joy, integrity, and impact.

In connecting with each of them, my hope is that you'll also appreciate more of your unique leadership qualities and feel inspired to put them into practice in your own valuable way.

It's difficult to create an inclusive environment that invites the valuable talents of others if we're not more acquainted and confident in our own capacities. So, this book is for you if you're ready, willing, and available to explore a way of seeing yourself and also seeing others… through the lens of appreciation for what's easily observed and also to tune our lenses to be able to observe what's often missed or overlooked.

With our vantage points more primed for clarity, we become more powerful agents of positive change for the well-being of everyone… not by changing who we are, but by becoming more of who we truly are.

It begins by excavating and practicing more of our shared humanity and realizing that we can each be a leader by the way we choose to lead our lives.

This is your time; this is our time.
We can do big, bright, bold, beautiful things when we're nourished, strong, and supported by fellow service-driven leaders.

May you continue to shine and be supported as your path unfolds. And again, welcome. I'm so happy that our paths have crossed.

2

REDEFINING AND REFINING TERMS

FOR THE PURPOSE OF CLARITY
OF LANGUAGE USED FROM THE RESEARCH
AND IN THIS FRAMEWORK

1. Joy: the internal state that allows service-driven leaders to feel a high level of integrity, confidence, trust in their capacities, concentrate, communicate more effectively, collaborate with others, think of innovative solutions, and engage in meaningful actions.

As 'Abdu'l-Baha explained in 1912 in *Paris Talks*:

"Joy gives us wings! In times of joy our strength is more vital, our intellect keener, and our understanding less clouded. We seem better able to cope with the world and to find our sphere of usefulness."

2. Leaders: People who choose to live their lives to cultivate their innate gifts, express their humanity, and take actions that improve their own lives and improve the lives of others.

They believe that having a legacy known for making a positive impact and service to others is a meaningful metric of success for a fulfilling, satisfying life.

This is not simply defined by birthright, title, position of power or influence, or social standing.

People who discover and decide to show up in one's life with integrity, strive to stay in alignment with their values, have a vision for how to contribute to a healthier, happier, more united world.

They choose to be part of the constructive forces that build, connect, heal, support, uplift, encourage, teach, accompany, learn, grow, and include, rather than the deconstructive forces that knowingly tear down, break apart, terrorize, divide, segregate, harm, hurt, or hate.

3. Leadership: the posture of learning how to make each day better than yesterday, refining steps mindfully, cultivating gifts and strengths consciously, embodying beliefs and expressing values respectfully, deciding that improving the quality of life for our fellow humans is a noble and worthy use of time, energy, and resources.

Leading by example and inspiring others to develop their humanity and qualities to become the best version of themselves.

3

THE LEADERSHIP STYLE OF ELEVATING ENVIRONMENTS AND NOURISHING SPACES

As I walk, as I walk
The universe is walking with me
In beauty it walks before me
In beauty it walks behind me
In beauty it walks below me
In beauty it walks above me
Beauty is on every side
Traditional Navajo Prayer

The environment is where we all meet;
where all have a mutual interest;
it is the one thing all of us share.
Lady Bird Johnson

One of the first conditions of happiness
is that the link between man and nature
shall not be broken.
Leo Tolstoy

A SPECIAL PLACE IN THE WORLD
THAT INSPIRED THIS CHAPTER

This Leadership Style always reminds me of a moment when I was living in Zhenjiang, China. After I finished graduate school in Philadelphia in 2003, I was serving in the role of a Cultural Ambassador for Pearl S. Buck International until 2005.

This was my first time living outside of the United States. I had lived away from my family during my years of university, but they were only a two-hour train ride away on Amtrak.

So, to move to the other side of the world - with a 12- hour time zone difference - and away from my family, friends, community, and everything I was familiar with, was a huge leap for me.

During my fourth week of living in this ancient city, everything looked unknown and everything felt outside of my comfort zone

I was very early in learning Mandarin — although there was something about the language that I found fascinating and so logical — and getting acclimated to a new chapter of my life.

In a few short months between finishing university with a Master's Degree and boarding a plan to China, I went from feeling the most educated and independent that I had been up to that point in my life, to suddenly being completely illiterate and not being able to accomplish the most basic of tasks, such as purchase a bus ticket, ask for directions, or read a menu to order food from a restaurant.

It was quite humbling and created the conditions to learn so much in my new environment, yet also challenge my compassion and patience with myself.

Most things felt unfamiliar, and I was learning about myself and how to adapt to my new surroundings.

On many occasions, I felt as though I was learning how to do everything again from scratch, such as speaking a new language that I couldn't yet read, learning cultural norms and new ways of greeting people, a different currency, work and holiday schedules, public transportation, types of food, sizes of clothing and shoes, how to mail a letter, and the list could continue for pages.

On the other hand, being new to a space awakened all of my senses and I paid attention to opportunities to savor the flavors of my new city. I made new friends, served some of the most adorable children I had ever met, learned how to dance traditional dances, had classes with a masterful classical musician to play the bamboo flute, learned Qi Gong from a 92 year old Traditional Chinese Medicine physician, learned how to make authentic Zhenjiang cuisine — including Spring Festival dumplings — which I can still make, enjoyed beautiful dishes filled with handmade noodles, hiked the tallest mountains I've ever seen, marveled at the beauty of nature that still takes my breath away, and so many other adventures that make me eternally grateful for the opportunity to live and work there.

One of my favorite spots was a teahouse right in the heart of Zhenjiang, a city located along the Yangtze River and just a 3-hour train ride from Shanghai.

I remember the first time I walked into this particular teahouse. With the many teahouses that are available to enjoy throughout the country, this one instantly became my favorite. There was a long walkway to enter, with a koi pond and the sound of a fountain near the entrance that followed you as you walked to the main area.

There was soft er-hu music playing in the distance. The er-hu is a 2-stringed instrument that is commonly played in China. There was a fragrance in the air that I couldn't identify initially, but it drew me in like a cartoon character that just caught the smell of a mouth-watering dish.

Everything about this teahouse felt inviting, felt peaceful, and conveyed that all was well.

From the welcome hostess to the manager who respectfully bowed to us with his hands pressed against his heart, the environment had the feeling of familiarity — although I had never been there before. It felt like I had just walked into the home of a great friend who was happy to have me there.

I felt confident to practice speaking the Mandarin phrases that I had learned over the last few weeks. There was a feeling to freely communicate and a belief that we'd be able to understand each other, even though we were meeting for the first time.

The manager greeting continued as he walked with my small group of colleagues and showed us the various places we could sit — either in the main area or in a private room with our own table and choices of food.

As he smiled, he said that he was 'happy to have the opportunity to meet friends from other countries so we can appreciate each other's cultures' and 'enjoy this moment in time' and that he 'hopes that we would enjoy the tea and food that's prepared with much thoughtfulness'.

After sampling many types of tea that evening, I found that the jasmine pearl tea was extraordinary. It had a light, lovely fragrance that reminded me of a garden I used to visit with my grandparents outside of Philadelphia.
The taste of the jasmine tea enhanced the flavors of all the dishes I tried, and instead of competing, it complemented them.

Every time I visited this lovely space, I felt like I could have a pause from any of the stressful, challenging, overwhelming feelings. For within these walls — and with these lovely hosts — there was a recentering and recalibrating feeling that we all need at times.

Even though it wasn't a place where I lived, it always provided a space that felt like a peaceful home... a home of ease and calm, of tranquility and reconnection.

NICKNAME FOR THIS LEADERSHIP STYLE

After meeting and working with hundreds of individuals who represent this Leadership Style, I've found that they can — each in their own unique way — contribute to making any environment where they spend time feel like a nourishing home.

So, I affectionately nickname this Leadership Team as:
The Gardeners and Respite Makers

Let's check out why.

BELIEFS, VALUES, VANTAGE POINTS,
AND UNIQUE QUALITIES OF THIS LEADERSHIP TEAM

Not everyone grew up in spaces that felt peaceful, nourishing, or nurturing. While all people benefit from their needs being supported — at any age — these unique leaders have an inner vantage point that makes it clear to see the importance of people spending time in healthy, encouraging environments.

This group of leaders seem to have a gallon-measure capacity to see potential opportunities to improve the quality of any space they happen to observe. This can include personal or professional spaces, such as: houses or apartments, day care centers, schools, community centers, hospitals, offices, parks, neighborhoods, buildings, university campuses, vehicles, clinics, and restaurants.

They believe that there is a dynamic relationship between people and the spaces where they spend their lives.
They feel a clear awareness that the quality of an environment impacts the quality of life of a person, and that people impact the quality of an environment.

What's essential for them is to be able to improve or refine the way spaces consistently look, feel, and function.

They experience a lot of joy and feel engaged with their strengths by elevating the quality of spaces where life is happening.
This is because they understand that welcoming, kind, encouraging environments are a significant factor for the quality of how people live. Once these needs are tended to, people have a better chance of learning and remembering, concentrating and focusing, resting and sleeping, creating and innovating, healing and recovering, playing and laughing.

This Leadership Team cares deeply about people having spaces to spend time in that feel the way a true home should feel... safe to grow and develop the innate talents and possibilities that are within every human being.

They realize at a fundamental level that people have a harder time developing all of the aspects of their emotional, physical, psychological, mental capacities when they're constantly in spaces that are crushing them with criticism, condemnation, chastisement, or violence.

All industries and communities in the world benefit when there are people who lead their lives with this Leadership Style and vantage point clear and trained, for they are helping to reverse the many consequences of harsh conditions that don't help people feel safe in their own skin.

CONTRIBUTIONS TO COMMUNITIES AND CULTURES

Representative of this Leadership Style stand out in many ways.

They naturally look at a situation, challenge, or goal through a "microscopic", detail-oriented lens.

They notice the details and subtle elements that are often overlooked or seen as a "luxury" or "final touch".

Their Leadership Lens is primed to see the details with clarity and obvious definition.

They help to remove the stigma or fear of making mistakes.

They encourage people to be patient with themselves while they're in a learning process.

They don't require perfection in order to make progress.

They help a space feel lighter and with less stress that pulverizes a person's confidence to try new things or advance beyond their comfort zone.

They are aware that stress is a part of life, but in their presence stress doesn't have to be the primary fuel of progress.

They shift the focus away from stress and scarcity, which tends to feel like driving on a road with sudden speed bumps.

Conversely, they tend to present more encouraging words and helpful options that make the learning, growing, designing process feel smoother. This helps people step out of being in a survival mode and experience new conditions that are supportive of a new posture.

This Leadership Style is passionate about contributing to the quality of passing knowledge — but just as importantly — about also passing on kindness and consideration about how to implement the knowledge in meaningful ways.

They desire to embody qualities that enable as many people as possible to live well, and for them, it all begins with enriching the quality of the various spaces that humans spend their time in.

They believe that everyone has the need to be in a healthy environment, starting at birth. When children are being raised in places where they feel cared about, valued, appreciated, accompanied as they learn, encouraged to try again and again, learning by the good example of the people in their spaces, they are being set up to succeed.
This doesn't mean that life will become perfect and there won't be challenges throughout their lifetimes, but it does seem that it helps young people grow into adults who are more patient, kind, thoughtful, proactive, confident, caring, and resilient to overcome challenges.

So, they understand that people have a better chance of being happier, healthier, more vibrant, more successful, more grounded, more compassionate, and more thoughtful when they spend time in nourishing spaces.

In a way, they serve as gardeners who realize that the most capable seeds need to be planted in soil that is nutrient-dense, balanced, safe, and healthy.

Then the seeds require consistent care with the appropriate combination of sunshine, fresh air and water, and the removal of harmful weeds in order to nurture their growth from seeds into thriving plants.

This is the way that plants naturally grow into their potential from the support of their environments… and people have this similar need.

A HERO'S STORY

The first person in my life who made a deep impression on me by embodying the Leadership Style of Elevating Environments and Nourishing Spaces is someone I've talked about many times over the years.

The way she leads her life is not something she learned by earning a degree or by completing years of an internship or residency.

Her Leadership Style turned out to be already quite natural and impactful when she was only 17 years old.

We met when I was going into my freshman year of high school, and it was during the summer music program in August.

I had been part of the middle school band and was always excited to see the Harrisburg High Marching Band dance and perform in parades, at homecoming, and Battle of the Bands.

My high school was known for the unique style of marching band that continues the tradition of HBCU's (Historically Black Colleges and Universities) in the United States.

Some marching bands in our area adopted a style that was more traditional to the military. Ours had some of those elements, as well, and also incorporated more popular and old-school music that had everyone in the audience moving and dancing. Our high school band had choreography and a drum line that made my little middle school heart so excited. I just thought it would be so fun to be part of a group that were so united in their coolness that it inspired everyone else to dance and have fun.

There was a happiness that I couldn't describe, but I had this feeling that if I was part of that group of musicians, high school wouldn't be as big of a leap into the unknown.

There was just one "little" problem: I couldn't dance.
In fact, I participated in one dance class when I was six years old, and it was — let's say this very clearly — a disaster. I had no idea how to move my feet, ankles, legs, arms, or shoulders the way the teacher was instructing the group. I stood clueless as she called out movements for us to do, watching the other girls accomplish every single movement like it was no big deal.

Yet, I felt paralyzed. The more I tried, the more awkward I looked, and the worse I felt.

"Why can't you just move your ankles? Here, like this. Just try. It isn't hard. Look at everyone else."
My teacher looked exhausted as she kept trying to move my limbs the right way.
I just couldn't figure out how to do the movements and I could feel her frustration with me, especially since all the other six girls in the room were doing everything so smoothly.

"Maybe I'll practice and be able to do it next time," I thought to myself, since I didn't want to give up. She wrapped up the class and dismissed us to get our coats, so we'd be ready to meet our parents.

Then I heard her feedback to my father, and I remember it like it was last week: *"You have a sweet girl, but dancing isn't for her. She's the least coordinated child I've ever seen. Maybe enroll her in another activity, because dance is not for her."*

I never went back to her class — instead started playing soccer and learned musical instruments well — but still remembered that "dance wasn't for me".

Although seven years later when I was 13 and enamored with the prospect of being able to play and perform in the marching band, I had a decision to make.
I could either hide in the fear of not knowing how to dance — a skill that was essential to the entire activity — and end up missing out on having so much fun like the students I'd been watching for years.

Or I could decide to go for It, learn the music, and somehow — perhaps by osmosis — magically transform into someone who has rhythm and can learn choreography and look cool doing it.

In that moment, it was a biggest leap of trust that everything could align and come together well. I decided to go for it and do my best.

So, the first week of band rehearsals went well. I'm learning the songs, making new friends, getting to know my new band instructor. Everything feels so much more important because high school competitions and performances are so much more visible. In my mind, more visibility meant more voices of criticism. Half-time shows at football games are packed with people who are looking forward to the songs we're going to play. There were songs by Earth, Wind & Fire which made everyone stand up, sing along, and celebrate this music together.

Then the second week was dedicated to learning the choreography. It felt like it was going to be fun and I was getting excited at what we were going to learn. There was some apprehension also, but 60% excitement felt like a win.

That was the case until I heard someone say:

"Every movement counts. Every movement needs to be precise and in unison. Every person in the stands should see each movement well. We need to move as one. Anything that sticks out makes the whole group look off."

That was it. I felt like I totally did not belong there. Then the negative self-talk ran wild in my head:

"What on earth was I thinking?

I can't do this! I'm going to mess up! And worst of all, I'm going to make everyone else look bad because I can't dance and I have no coordination. And everyone else looks like they have an extra dose of coordination and rhythm. Why did I come here? I'm just wasting everyone's time and taking up a spot that could be for someone else. I can't let them see me and my uncoordinated feet. They need coordinated feet!

It's probably best if I just slip out when everyone's outside on our break. How can I get out of this without anyone realizing I'm gone?"

Before I knew it, the break was over, and we were put into four parallel lines to begin learning the dance steps. My heart was pounding, and I was sweating so much more than what was necessary. I wanted to disappear, but everyone could see me. I was one of the only people with light skin. I'm already standing out and now it's going to be terrible because I can't do the necessary choreography.

The more worried I got, the worse my attempts became. We weren't even doing the more complicated steps yet. These were still the basics, and I was awful. At least, the way it felt to me was I had now destroyed any possibility of being cool with these amazing dancers.

I could feel the upper classmen behind me, probably wondering what on earth I was doing there. I just wanted to disappear.

Then something happened that changed everything. The very cool drum major who was an amazing dancer that I was trying to follow came up to me. I realized that she had been watching me fumble and look sad. She gave a subtle head nod and gestured for me to follow her. Just me.

I assumed this was her kind way of gently asking me to leave — much like my dance teacher from when I was younger. I thanked her for letting me go early so I could catch the bus without all the other students on it so I wouldn't feel embarrassed. Once I started taking my instrument apart so I could collect my things, she stopped me.

"You're not leaving, sweetie. Follow me. Let's get you together."

She proceeded to take me into the drum room — away from everyone else — so I could let my guard down and tell her what was happening. I felt like crying and felt so overwhelmed at my lack of skill and courage. I didn't want her to see me fail, especially because she was someone who I looked up to.

She asked me, *"So what's the problem with the dance moves? You were doing great with learning all the songs."*

"I have no rhythm and dance isn't for me," I recited word-for-word, like I had been told.

"Do you know what your problem is?" she continued without appearing to believe what I had said, *"You're trying to dance from your head, and you're supposed to dance from your heart."*

A huge sigh of relief suddenly appeared. No one had ever told me that before. I didn't really understand what that meant, but it sounded true, and I became curious.

Plus, I trusted her because she seemed to have a switch that allowed her to dance with incredible precision and with so much light-heartedness.

Watching her dance made me feel like I could do it too… if I only knew how. Then she showed me.

"First, stop thinking and just take a deep breath. Good."

I followed her lead.

"Now again. Another deep breath. Good, there you go."

I followed her lead. My throat didn't ache any longer from holding back tears and my chest didn't feel tense. She was being so kind to me and I didn't know why, but I went with it because it seemed to flow from her with so much ease and grace.

She asked me to close my eyes and feel my heartbeat. Then, she tapped the bass drum that was hanging next to her on a shelf. She started making a beat and it was at the same pace as my heartbeat. She was helping me discover that I, in fact, do have rhythm. I just needed to be reminded of what it felt like and move in harmony with it.

After a few moments, I felt calm and relaxed, forgetting how tense and embarrassed I had been feeling five minutes before.

It wasn't long before she got me to feel steady and ready to take another attempt at the choreography, but in micro-steps. With her, there was no rush and no judgement. She only spoke with the belief that I could get there, I just needed to learn at a different pace. She didn't allow me to judge or belittle myself.

Instead, she transformed that small drum room to feel like the safest, most abundant place where we could figure out anything that was difficult. What had been an obstacle that felt impossible for years suddenly felt not only possible, but tangible.

Once we practiced the choreography a few times together, there was a point where she noticed I was smiling and having fun. No longer afraid of making mistakes, I could allow myself to have a posture in which the movements could flow. It wasn't exactly as cool as her dancing, but I felt confident enough to keep learning.

When my whole system seemed to have been emotionally rebooted, she winked at me and said, "*I think you're ready to join the group again. You got this.*"

I paused with a little bit of anxiety because there were so many pairs of eyes outside, and it would feel different than the cozy nook of safety that she created for me.

"*You got this. And I got you,*" she replied, giving me one more boost of confidence so I wouldn't feel alone. I believed her.

When the same drum line started playing again and the same choreography was about to start, I felt different. I felt connected to and encouraged by someone who wanted me to succeed, not to be paralyzed by fear. Her accompaniment and support meant so much, and then she gave me another wink, so I knew I wasn't alone. The huge space outdoors suddenly felt at safe and sound as the small drum room we had just been in.

That was the day I found my rhythm, my love for dance, and friends who created a space for me to feel like I was good to show up as I am.

I'll never forget the look on people's faces when I went in the drum room without knowing how to dance and came out 15 minutes later moving like a whole different person. I felt like I had found a space to learn, grow, and develop parts of myself that hadn't had the opportunity or support to gain strength.

Everything remains dormant until it's activated.

It was also the first time in my first 14 years of living when I heard the words, *"Ok Jaleh! We see you. You're one of us."*

There wasn't a hint of criticism. In that moment — in that space Aliya helped create — I felt both seen **and** a true sense of belonging. Safe was no longer synonymous with invisible. In that moment, being visible **and** feeling safe became possible. This was all because of how Aliya chose to show up, reflecting so many qualities that she embodies naturally and powerfully… just by being her authentic self.

IMPACT & INSIGHTS

Because of Aliya, I found a place where I could learn, be imperfect, be willing to learn and grow, and feel comfortable in my own skin.

This experience activated a new sense of identity in which I didn't have to believe that challenges of my past determine my current capacities. I no longer had to accept the criticisms of others as the truth of what's possible.
Having patience with ourselves during the process of learning a new skill or talent is a great strength to train. Greatness requires training, and training requires imperfections to be seen.

How wonderful it is that the world is filled with people like Aliya who have this Leadership Style so that there can be more spaces that nourish and empower people while they're developing their strengths.

He that plants trees loves others besides himself.
Dr. Thomas Fuller

SOME WELL-KNOWN PEOPLE
WHO REPRESENT THIS LEADERSHIP STYLE

"Create the highest, grandest vision possible for your life, because you become what you believe."
Oprah Winfrey

"Who we are cannot be separated from where we're from."
"People don't rise from nothing… It is only by asking where they are from that we can unravel the logic behind who succeeds and who doesn't."
"Success is not a random act. It arises out of a predictable and powerful set of circumstances and opportunities."
Malcolm Gladwell

THE NUTRIENT THAT MIRRORS QUALITIES
OF THIS LEADERSHIP STYLE

Omega 3 is the nutrient that I associate with the Leadership Style of Elevating Environments and Nourishing Spaces, not because these individuals enjoy walnuts, salmon, and chia seeds, but rather because of how these people function in an organization much like Omega 3.

This nutrient is essential to the healing process by reducing inflammation when it strikes. Omega 3 also provides a balance to hormone levels, as well as helping the brain to function well.

If inflammation persists, tissues in the body do not heal.
Much like the way people function together, heightened irritation or anger can drastically change the dynamic in professional, public, and personal spaces.

When tempers continue to run hot or when frustrations aren't alleviated with helpful solutions, people tend to not communicate effectively nor think at optimal levels. When people aren't able to feel steady, it creates a thicker barrier for their talents to shine.

This makes the goals and objectives more difficult to achieve and can create conditions in which people seek out other options that would feel more attractive and satisfying.

The "Omega 3 leaders" of a community or organization can create conditions and environments that are set up for successful consultations, problem solving, solution-seeking endeavors, implementing useful details, training new or updated skills, overcoming challenges, and resilience after unforeseen difficulties have occurred.

REFLECTION QUESTIONS TO PRACTICE
THIS LEADERSHIP QUALITY:

1. How do you feel when you're in an environment that has too much "inflammation" (criticism, anger, frustration, resentment, fear, etc.) in the conversations or in people's actions?

2. What would you say and do that could make spaces you spend time in feel more nurturing or more encouraging for people to be in?

TREASURE HUNT INVITATION
TO TAKE INSPIRED ACTION

Now that you've thought of some of the conditions in the environment that help you feel good in your space, you're invited to implement one of your ideas into the space where you work, live, visit, shop, or connect with people.
(This can be virtual spaces and in-person spaces.)

Bonus: Think of ways to make the space nourishing and encouraging for you AND for the others who you interact with.

4

THE LEADERSHIP STYLE OF EXPRESSION AND COMMUNICATION

NEVER DOUBT THAT A SMALL GROUP OF THOUGHTFUL, COMMITTED CITIZENS CAN CHANGE THE WORLD; INDEED, IT IS THE ONLY THING THAT EVER HAS.

Margaret Mead

The art of communication
is the language of leadership.
James Humes

Communication is the lifeline of any relationship.
Elizabeth Bourgeret

Communication is the solvent of all problems and
is the foundation for personal development.
Peter Shepherd

Good communication is the bridge
between confusion and clarity.
Nat Turner

Communication works for those who work at it.
John Powell

Communication is the sister of leadership.
John Adair

A SPECIAL PLACE IN THE WORLD
THAT INSPIRED THIS CHAPTER

When I was in my senior year of high school, I decided to write a 10-year list. This was a type of mini bucket list describing things I wanted to achieve, subjects I wanted to learn about, and places I wanted to visit before my 28th birthday.

One of the places on my list was to experience New Delhi, India. Ten years passed and I had traveled to some incredible places, but India was not yet one of them, and there was a space in my passport still waiting for a stamp from that ancient land. So, visiting India was added to my next 10-year list to focus on before my 38th birthday.

Through a combination of circumstances and conversations, friendships were made and introductions happened. Doors of opportunity opened. I received an invitation to speak at a global economic conference in New Delhi - which was scheduled for just three weeks after my 38th birthday.

Some of the people I met at that event have remained good friends of mine, and we've visited each other in our respective cities and countries.

The following year, I was scheduled to present at a global conference in New Delhi again, and one of my dear friends offered me a lovely invitation to stay a few days after the event finished so I could see more parts of the city, as well as her hometown.

Her father picked me up from the conference venue and drove me to their family's home outside of the city.

We spoke about our backgrounds, our families, our interests, the origin of our names, how much we enjoy meeting people from various backgrounds, and how much Persian culture and Indian culture are inter-connected.

When we arrived to their home, we were greeted by the smiles and hugs of the family members, as well as the rich aroma of spices overflowing from the kitchen. I felt like I stepped into a five-star restaurant. The table was being set with small plates and colorful napkins. The deep hues of oranges, tangerines, pomegranate reds, pistachio greens, and canary yellows turned the wooden table into a buffet of colors. It was a feast for the eyes. Every dish enhanced the brilliant colors of the others surrounding it.

I appreciated the details that were thoughtfully arranged, which conveyed without words but in actions: "welcome to our home".

The surprising thing was that I absolutely felt at home. Although it was my first time stepping into this space and meeting my friend's family members, each person in the family communicated that they were happy to have me there.

Then another perfume hit my olfactory senses and I got so happy at the realization of what was to come.

"Jaleh, do you like Indian chai?"

I tried to keep my composure polite and calm, since they just met me and didn't realize that I'm a serious tea fan.
"Oh yes, I like it very much," were the words I said, but in my mind, I was thinking, *"This is the most amazing smell so I'm sure it's going to be the best chai... and if there was a pool made of chai, I'd dive in and be in my happy place."*

I'm glad I didn't say any of this out loud since it sounds quite ridiculous, but needless to say, the chai was delicious, and I enjoyed multiple cups throughout my stay there.
One of the sweetest parts of enjoying that specially prepared tea was the quality of the conversations around their beautiful table.

There were so many heart-warming stories about how the parents met, about the matriarch of the family, how much I've wanted to visit India since I was a teenager, our passion for work and service, creativity and meditation, intercultural relationships and marriages, and how I got to know a bit about Indian culture from my childhood and university friends and roommate.

The Leadership Style of Expression and Communication always reminds me of this experience in my life because we all had open hearts and minds to express ourselves, listen and learn from other people's experiences, and communicate across so many interesting and diverse backgrounds.

The outcome was more connection, appreciation, respect and unity.

NICKNAME FOR THIS LEADERSHIP STYLE

After working with hundreds of people who represent this Leadership Style, I've realized that they can — each in their own unique way — contribute to priming conversations to lead to more understanding, respect, and awareness.

So, I affectionately nickname this Leadership Team as:
Bridge-builders and Amplifier of Unifying Voices

Let's explore how.

BELIEFS, VALUES, VANTAGE POINTS, AND UNIQUE QUALITIES OF THIS LEADERSHIP TEAM

I've worked with hundreds of people who share this Leadership Style, and I'm in awe of how much they have in common with each other when they communicate. They consistently said that they believe people can continue expanding the depth of awareness and breadth of understanding, regardless of the starting position.

They adopted a certainty that when the quality of communication improves, this starts to change the tides of improving relationships, community, businesses, schools, job performance, and the culture of an organization. According to their perspective, every voice can add to their understanding of people's lived experiences.

This widens their spectrum of realizing how human beings operate, how they feel, what helps them feel respected and free to share their voices, and ultimately be seen as worthy of respect and valued.

They desire to improve the quality of expression and communication in order to deepen more people's understanding of themselves and of each other. They realize that many people in the world are not encouraged to use their voices — either due to many reasons connected to their class, socio-economic background, age, experience, gender, culture, nationality, traditions, title, role, status, etc.

"Every voice can add to my awareness beyond my own lived experience, which is limited by geography, resources, time, culture, etc. Therefore, every voice — including my own — has inherent value." This tends to be what is shared as a collective value from representatives of this Leadership Style.

They are dedicated to fostering a culture and community that is curious to understand what is at the heart of what people are needing to express.

They develop the skill of active and thoughtful listening.
They try to lean in to all of the aspects of expression to understand what is said in words, and also in tone, pauses, body language, facial expressions.

In this manner, they create an environment that helps people feel safe to share their opinions, their ideas for achieving a goal, and their experiences that can be helpful to moving the needle forward.

When this Leadership Style team is part of a project, they seek to find the most helpful, productive, and profound layers of understanding in order to implement meaningful solutions.

They tend to not get stuck in unhelpful banter or venting sessions. Rather, they ask questions that allow everyone involved to offer the ideas that nourish the roots of the vision and goals of the group.

"We can learn difficult, complex, challenging things. There are solutions to all the problems we need to solve.
Finding solutions requires patience and presence to hear, perceive, and respect all the voices who are sharing the best they have to offer."

They also see the benefit of storytelling in order to share meaningful experiences and express patterns of what people currently need.

Because they value quality communication that is designed to activate more awareness for everyone involved, they embody and serve as an example of understanding and respect.

These leaders don't require everyone to agree or immediately understand every other person's lived experience.
However, they do create the conditions in which everyone can be treated with respect when they share their voices.
This cultivates a culture of learning from each other that feels more accessible, enjoyable, and eventually more natural.

One of their notable traits is how they help remove the fear and guilt of not knowing how to interact with so many different lived experiences and the wide spectrum of knowledge.

One of their greatest desires and gifts is to help people — themselves included — not feel alone or isolated in a challenging situation or learning process.
They strive to close the gap of understanding that often divides people and can weaken the bonds between people. They realize at a fundamental level that a community cannot be strong when people don't know how or aren't encouraged to express themselves and communicate with others well.

They work very well with the Leadership Style of Relationship & Community-Building because they both contribute to the fabric of a healthy and thriving community.

This leadership team desire to be a force for bridge-building so the process of developing a higher degree of awareness and respectful communication can be successful and sustainable.

To read is to gain wings for the world.
Unknown

CONTRIBUTIONS TO COMMUNITIES AND CULTURES

Every Leadership Style has a unique perspective that can add a much-needed element to solutions. This Leadership Style has a unique vantage point, which is oriented to notice meaningful details. People who have this Leadership Style are generally primed to see the details and nuances that are often overlooked. They look beyond the superficial level of a situation, and thoughtfully search for deeper, more profound meanings of what is being expressed, what's being shared, what the current conversation is focusing on.

I think of these leaders as X-ray machines. They realize that there are important elements involved in a situation that require special attention and skill. They don't shy away from topics that have a great complexity or multi-layered understanding required.

When they're in situations in which the focus is on the big picture possibility and not making space for the well-designed details, conversations to ensure everyone is on the same page, and valuable refinements to be part of the process, this is when these leaders shine.

They point out opportunities to communicate, redefine, or express the important points in a way so that there is a united collective vision, clarity of the path, and well-understood roles that each person can contribute their skills and talents.

A HERO'S STORY

One of my favorite leaders to talk about is my childhood best friend. We'll call him Ali.

We met when we were 11 years old, and our birthdays are two weeks apart. We were both in college-prep classes, relatively short compared to the rest of our circle of friends, athletic, and loved movies and music.

His love for music exceeded anyone else I knew. He played musical instruments, he wrote music, he wrote lyrics and rhymes, he created poems that conveyed the essence of an emotion or feeling. He wrote about creativity, struggle, courage, resilience, searching for meaning, and being a young Black man who had passions and dreams for the future. Although we looked, sounded, expressed ourselves differently — in almost every way — we always had a connection that was not based on being the same. We didn't try to change each other. We had different things that lit us up with happiness, that annoyed us, that inspired us, that motivated us, that scared us, that made us feel safe, and that gave us courage.

We did have a number of values in common: family, community, learning how to think well, pursuing a quality education, creativity, imagination, exploring the world around us, and spending time with people we trust.

With all of the intersections of diversity we both represented — internal and external — there was always a spacious field to connect and understand each other.
Our discussions from high school and college are still some of the most profound, provocative, memorable, and character-building conversations of my life.

We spoke from logic and reason, as well as emotion and feeling. We both believed in each other's intelligence and respected our individual learning process.

Both of us graduated with honors — although he was the salutatorian and gave a speech that brought the entire concert hall to their feet. I was so honored to be his friend, and I knew he'd go on to continue making everyone who loved him proud.

We were all better for knowing him, and he always challenged me to not stay small and go bigger than I was usually comfortable.
He had a habit of asking me why I was doing something or what I truly wanted — so I would say it out loud and not keep it to myself. There was something important to him to remind me that I have a voice so I should use it and not follow some cultural tendencies of holding back.

With him, I felt this freedom to say exactly what I wanted, what I meant, what I had a problem with, and what I dared to dream about. He filled the space with this powerful permission to express what's needing to be expressed.

Once we started freshman year at our respective universities, I missed sitting next to him at class and going over homework assignments together. Not having his presence on campus left a void.

There were so many lessons my first semester supplied me — some more challenging than others. Some days felt like a rude awakening, and I had to relearn and remember the valuable vantage point that Ali always carried with him:

"Focus on learning in a way so you can understand what's really happening and what matters the most."

What I didn't plan for was learning how to understand a challenging event that had nothing to do with what I was learning in my science-heavy courses.

I was living on campus in a dorm with suite-style design. There were four rooms in each suite, and I was fortunate to have some great roommates who got along well. On an early Wednesday morning, my roommate got up early to take an Organic Chemistry exam and I didn't have my calculus class until 9am. My alarm went off at 8am and I hit the snooze instantly to get another precious ten minutes of sleep.

I went right back to sleep and, minutes later, I was jolted awake by the loudest "BOOM" I had ever heard and the subsequent shattering of glass. It was as though I had felt the BOOM punch me and my system vibrated with adrenaline.

Not knowing what caused the blast and the crashing noise of glass, I started to look around my dorm room that was located on the sixth floor.

The wooden frame of my bunk bed also seemed to have been affected by the blast.
There were pieces of wood spread all over the floor and small area carpet. My heart was racing, and I thought of action movies I had seen when people get away from the windows in case of a shooting.

"But I'm on the top floor of the dorm. How could someone be shooting up here?" I thought to myself and then tried to reason with the situation.

"I'm ok, I'm safe. Maybe it was a tree branch? No, the trees along the street aren't that high. Maybe it was a car backfiring? No, that would crack the window and break my bunk bed."

Nothing made sense from the floor until I looked up and saw the window. There was a small circular shape that had pierced the glass and cracked the rest of the window — like a spider web that goes from the center and fills the rest of the space. Then I put all the pieces together. It was a bullet. It was a bullet that traveled a path through my window, through my bed frame, through my mattress, through my closet door, and landed in my right sneaker.

I went cold and silent and raced out of the room. Thank goodness none of my suite mates were there. I heard more gun shots, but I didn't know what they struck.

"Please don't let anyone get hurt. Maybe I'm the only one who knows this is happening."

Luckily, the bullet didn't touch me, although I felt its path as it went through the mattress I was laying on.

"I'm safe. I'm ok. I gotta call security. I have to make sure people stay away from the windows."

Fortunately, the shooter fired 3 shots to 3 dorm rooms, and I was the only one who was actually inside. Most of the students had been at the early morning exam, so they didn't know anything happened until they came back to the dorm and it was surrounded by police, detectives, and personnel.

After being interviewed by the detectives — feeling so numb I could say everything as though I was describing a TV show I had recently watched. The gentlemen kept looking at me like they wanted to reach out and give me a hug but wanted to be professional.

Finally, one officer said, *"I'm so sorry that this happened. We're gonna do everything we can to find the criminal who did this to you. You're just a kid… same age as my daughter. She's away at school, and you're away from your family. I'm sorry, kid."*

Another detective asked if there was anything he could do to make me feel better, and I felt so numb and cold, I appreciated him but couldn't think of one thing.

I just wanted to disappear into my regular schedule and go to class. I had a calculus exam on Friday, and I didn't want to miss it. I had a chemistry lab assignment due the next day, and how could I concentrate? Everyone on campus was talking about "the shooting" and about the "girl who was the only one who knows what happened".

It felt as though I was eavesdropping about myself, because most people didn't know I was that girl. I couldn't escape the chatter and the curiosities. There was a limit to how many times I wanted to recount the same story and say the same lines. While I didn't know most of the people very well — seeing their reaction of fear, sadness, or panic — I automatically adopted the role of saying things to help them feel better.

"I'm okay. We got lucky. It's going to be ok." I started to play these phrases like a broken record.

They couldn't say or do anything that would change what happened, nor change how I felt.
Everyone was processing the events of that day in their own way.
Everyone had a blend of emotions, reactions, and responses.

I also definitely did not want to go back to my dorm room. But where could I get some peace of mind and feel less cold? Who could I talk to who wouldn't make me feel like I was going to shatter into a thousand pieces — or they themselves break down?
Every time I closed my eyes, I couldn't sleep. I would hear the sounds of that morning again and feel that pulse of a punch.

I couldn't unwind my mind or relax my muscles. It felt like my nervous system was on "high alert".

Then, some days later, an unexpected phone call happened. It was Ali, deciding that we should check in and catch up.

Does he know what happened?

What amazing timing! I felt so relieved to hear his voice. The deep bass he spoke with always gave me the sense that everything was good. I just wanted to hear how he was doing.
I decided that I would keep the events from the shooting to myself. There was no need to worry him or upset him.

It's not like he can make these feelings go away.

I tried my best to sound my usually upbeat, happy voice. Although I thought I was doing a pretty decent job, there were cracks in my attempt that I couldn't hide or hold back. I tried clearing my throat, but it was no use. He knew my voice — my real voice — and was aware that something was off.

"So, what's up?" he said, giving me the space to say what really was on my mind and in my heart.

I deflected again and tried to steer the conversation to happier things and keep it light.

He was way too perceptive to fall for my pitiful attempt to fool my best friend. That's when I remembered, he's known me for much more time than my new friends, roommates, and professors.

I took a deep breath and said what I had been wanted to express for days. For the first time since the shooting, I didn't hold back. I allowed him to hear all of the vulnerability and uncertainty, the doubt and fear.

Because I knew him and trusted him, I just let it all be expressed. I didn't fear being seen as weak, unlikable, unpolished, uncensored.

He listened to everything I said. He allowed space for the pause and silence. He kept the conversation as wide open as I needed it to be. He said very little, but when he did speak, it was poetic magic.

He said that he needed a few minutes and he'd call me back as soon as he could — and that he was proud of me for *"saying all the things… that's what courage sounds like. Keep speaking with courage. I got you. Keep caring about people. Don't stop believing in people. Good people got your back."*

With that, we hung up but I was already looking forward to him calling me back. I figured he had another call or study group meeting. Although I already felt 10 pounds lighter after our conversation and feeling his support.

Then the phone rang again, and it was him. I think it was the first time I was genuinely smiling since that Wednesday morning.

"Hey! Ready for part 2?" I asked.

Ali didn't say anything.
Then I heard music playing with a really cool, powerful beat.

"This is for you. This is your song. Take it in. Breathe it in." He then continued to let the music play over the phone.

I took deep breaths and felt my heartbeat. The music led me back to myself — from feeling tense and on guard to feeling like I could breathe again.

We were both quiet as we listened to the music and the beats he had created so quickly.

"You're gonna be alright. And think of it like this: you had a bulletproof day. Not everyone can say that. Remember that."

Thank you, Ali. I remember. I remember all the time.

It's ok to express what's honest and true in our experience. It's valuable to have people who encourage our voices and care about understanding what we need.

The most important thing in communication
is to hear what isn't being said.
Peter Drucker

IMPACT & INSIGHTS

Ali taught me that it was ok to speak up and share my experience, even if other people hadn't gone through it themselves. Even if they didn't know how to relate or what to say, I could still use my voice and share how I felt and what I had seen. Obviously, it was scary for a variety of reasons and impacted me in many ways. Yet, the pain of feeling isolated or alone hurt in a different way.

My experience — although it was not the "normal" thing for a first-year college student to endure — didn't make me wrong or excluded. It didn't mean that I had to suffer in silence, nor disconnect from people simply because the maps of our lives were marked with different roads.

Even when I wanted to pretend that it didn't happen and ignore the entire situation so I could simply "move on", staying silent did not make me more equipped to move on or "to just get over it".

In the failed attempt to mute my voice and not share the events of that morning with my best friend, I was actually blocking someone who cared about me from offering the power of his kindness. It could have caused a barrier between me and other people because I was afraid of being misunderstood.

The truth became clear to me: isolating myself from people who are capable of care and compassion was not the solution.

Instead, authentically expressing myself to Ali led to my heartfelt needs being met simultaneously, and our connection and respect for each other grew even stronger.

Ali demonstrated that even when people don't experience the same events, they are able to offer understanding through thoughtful and loving words and actions. My community of loved ones understood that — although that Wednesday had finished when the clock struck midnight — it didn't feel over for me.

The progression of the calendar days didn't seem to suddenly make me feel unaffected. I still carried fear, panic, and sometimes hopelessness. Thankfully, these lovely people also had more awareness of my sensitivities to sudden, loud sounds and how that would sometimes trigger flashbacks, taking me back to that memorable day.

Despite the challenges, remembering that I wasn't a lone wolf, and that there were bridges created to connect to one another began melting away layers of fear.

By expressing my voice and communicating my situation, the people who cared about me showed up for me and reminded me that I am loved, and that in that moment in time… I was bulletproof.

I wasn't bulletproof because of a vest or special glass. Rather, because I was surrounded by people who wanted the best for me. They demonstrated their love through their kind-hearted actions, their kind eyes, their warm hugs, and thoughtful words and actions.

The goal is to clearly communicate that our connection and our presence in each other's lives are valuable, incalculable, and worthy of deeper understanding.

SOME WELL-KNOWN PEOPLE
WHO REPRESENT THIS LEADERSHIP STYLE

"All acts of kindness are lights in the war for justice."
"True power does not amass through the pain and suffering of others."
"We are all here to serve each other. At some point we have to understand that we do not need to carry a story that is unbearable.
We can observe the story, which is mental;
feel the story, which is physical;
let the story go, which is emotional;
then forgive the story, which is spiritual, after which we use the materials of it to build a house of knowledge."
Joy Harjo

"Ignorance is a cure for nothing.
Education must not simply teach work — it must teach life.
Men must not only know, they must act.
Children learn more from what you are than what you teach."
Strive for that greatness of spirit that measures life not by its disappointments but by its possibilities."
"Begin with art, because art tries to take us outside ourselves.
It is a matter of trying to create an atmosphere and context so conversation can flow back and forth and we can be influenced by each other."
W.E.B. Du Bois

*"Don't wait for permission to do something creative.
In narratives, you have to create the situations so that
the truth will come out."*
*"These stories deserve to be told — not as sociology, not as
spectacle, not as a singular event that happens every so often —
but regularly and purposefully as truth and as art on an ongoing
basis."*
Ava DuVernay

THE NUTRIENT THAT MIRRORS QUALITIES
OF THIS LEADERSHIP STYLE

The contribution of the Leadership Style of Communication & Expression reminds me of the nourishing qualities of zinc.

Zinc affects the human body in a multitude of ways, such as accelerating our immune system and preventing infections, fostering the process of healing wounds and treating burns, supporting thyroid function, from helping to prevent mental decline and heart disease to having well-functioning senses of taste and smell.

Zinc is vital for so many systems in our bodies to function, heal, and perform well.

Every person, family, community, team, organization, institution thrives when it is healthy and can recover when a difficulty or an "injury" occurs.

Robust learning, understanding, and awareness require quality communication and expression of ideas to be shared. Each voice houses possible methods of improvement to be implemented. When only certain voices are welcomed or respected — those are the only options available — and countless solutions and talents remain hidden. This Leadership Style team enhance the function and capacity of multiple facets of society to become stronger, more resilient, and prevent so many challenges.

These leaders actively pursue putting processes in place to hold the high standard of excellent expression and profound understanding that addresses the critical areas of growth.

Whenever this leadership quality is practiced consistently, it supports more success of an organization and provides a stronger community culture that values understanding and communicates effectively.

REFLECTION QUESTIONS
TO PRACTICE THIS LEADERSHIP QUALITY:

1. What is something about your life experience or current understanding that is valuable or important to you?

2. What is something that you understand — about yourself or your community or field of study — in a way that is **not** well-understood or known by everyone else?

TREASURE HUNT INVITATION
TO TAKE INSPIRED ACTION

Have a conversation with someone who was raised in a place, culture, or background that was not your own. Ask this person about a part of the culture, heritage, language, or tradition that helps her/him feel like a full, nourished, inspired, connected, whole human being?

As you listen attentively, focus on what you can appreciate, be curious about, value, respect, honor about her/his background and experience.
Allow yourself to be connected by what you have in common and appreciate about each other's diverse layers.

Invite the possibility that by seeing more of ourselves and each other, we get to build more bridges of understanding, rooted in genuine connection.

- You can take notes.

- You can draw a diagram or create a mind map.

- You can journal about your reflections of the conversation.

Ultimately, you're welcome to enjoy the process of learning, growing, and expanding your current depth of understanding by hearing the experience of someone else's path in life.

5

THE LEADERSHIP STYLE OF HUMANITY AND NOBLE ACTIONS

YOU MUST NOT LOSE FAITH IN HUMANITY.
HUMANITY IS LIKE AN OCEAN;
IF A FEW DROPS OF THE OCEAN ARE DIRTY,
THE OCEAN DOES NOT BECOME DIRTY

Mahatma Mohandas Karamchand Gandhi,
Lawyer & Nonviolent Resistance Leader

The greatness of humanity
is not in being human, but in being humane.

Mahatma Gandhi

The ultimate test of man's conscience
may be his willingness to sacrifice something
today for future generations whose words
of thanks will not be heard.

Gaylord Nelson

The darkness will try to overtake you
but just turn on the light, focus on the light,
hold onto the light.

Jon Batiste

A SPECIAL PLACE IN THE WORLD
THAT INSPIRED THIS CHAPTER

On my third trip to Geneva, Switzerland, I had the great opportunity to be a guest trainer with a dear mentor of mine for a group of highly respected leaders who have positions of service at the United Nations and World Health Organization.

Being in a room with people who sacrifice so much of their comfort and ease in order to help communities around the world facing some of the most difficult challenges was a huge honor for me.

Some of the participants were physicians and others were directors who help with logistical systems that supply food, clean water, medical supplies and professionals, safety and security, and countless other services that help people during times of crises — some natural disasters and others that were man-made.

After one of the sessions of this Leadership Conference, I was walking back to the hotel and stumbled upon a lovely little cafe overlooking the Rhône River. My brain was so full of stories and thoughts from the day, it seemed like a good idea to sit and process what I had just learned about this group of professionals.

Reflecting on the incredible projects the participants were currently responsible for and overseeing, I ordered a cup of lemon balm tea with honey.

I sat at my small table with my journal and pen, writing and recalling the moments shared that had elevated my respect for each of them. They each — in their own ways — cultivated this appreciation I have for the quality of courage. It seemed to flow from them naturally and effortlessly, but I realized a long time ago that people who make things appear easy have developed that skill and talent with a great amount of consistency and discipline.

They were a group that reflected consistent discipline in believing that a crisis can become a victory when people's humanity is safeguarded, invested in, encouraged, and believed in.

As I sat enjoying small sips of this aromatic tea, it felt as though I had just spent the day with a type of superhero that comic books haven't yet spotlighted. They had no capes nor fancy gadgets that they wore. They appeared to be "normal" people who enjoyed a coffee and pastry in the mornings. However, when they shared their experience during a previous mission, and what their biggest challenges were during a later mission, I found myself in awe of how much they each believed in humanity.

They each carried with them a flame of hope that was practical and understated.

Despite seeing — up close and very personal — some of the worst conditions that people were experiencing on a daily basis, they focused on what to do in order to change the current patterns of chaos.

Despite knowing that people were often at the root of these painful challenges, they didn't entertain the idea that things had to remain in a state of devastation. They were willing to put themselves in the places where people were suffering and be part of the solutions.
It didn't occur to them to give up or to turn a blind eye, nor to make excuses or to get caught up in the paralysis of inaction and debates.

On the contrary, they chose to be part of the fashioners and builders of communities — despite the amount of destruction and tragedy that was present.

I am forever grateful for the opportunity to serve that group of global leaders, for they turned up the intensity of hope that I have in humanity... by their example and from the experiences they've dedicated their lives to.

NICKNAME FOR THIS LEADERSHIP STYLE:
THE NURTURERS OF HOPE

After meeting and working with hundreds of individuals who represent this Leadership Style, I've found that they can — each in their own unique way — contribute to activating more hope in humanity and fostering processes that train our capacities to be worthy of the name human.

They infuse beliefs rooted in reciprocal respect and a shared sense of humanity into any environment where they spend their time.

So, I affectionately nickname this Leadership Team as.

The Beacons and Nurturers of Hope

Let's dive in to check out why.

BELIEFS, VALUES, VANTAGE POINTS,
AND UNIQUE QUALITIES OF THIS LEADERSHIP TEAM

One of the things that started to become clear after the ninth year of my research was that each Leadership Style has a unique vantage point. I started calling this element of the blueprint the "Leadership Lens", which refers to how a person most effortlessly and most effectively perceives things with clarity.

The lens of The Leadership Style of Humanity and Noble Actions is very different than the Styles covered thus far. That's because people with this Leadership Style have a vantage point that I describe in the framework as a Telescopic Lens. A telescopic leadership lens tends to naturally favor seeing big picture possibilities, despite the challenges that can be present and currently experienced by people. It's not that they ignore that challenges are part of the situation; however, they often believe that challenges are not stronger than the solutions.

They don't subscribe to the belief that humanity has to crumble, fall apart, or shrink in the face of challenges. They have a strong desire to be part of the solution — through both their words and their actions.

What's obvious to them can often be other people's blind spots of stress points of fear or doubt because they can:

- Focus to see the big picture goal that often dwells further along on a timeline and can require ten or more milestones of progress.

- Zoom out to see an expansive vision of possibilities that may be overlooked by the majority of people who are already absorbed in the challenging circumstance or situations.

- See the milestones and steps that are meaningful and transformational in order for progress to be achieved.

- Enjoy a vantage point that can reignite a spark of hope and desire to achieve big, bright, bold goals.

- Quicken the flame of hope and inspiration when they clearly communicate and express their ideas in a spirit of consultation. When they practice and develop this skill with others who have other strengths and vantage points — who may not yet live with the high degree of belief in human potential — their passion to develop our collective humanity encourages more people to enter the field of service with joy and energy.

CONTRIBUTIONS TO COMMUNITIES AND CULTURES

The Innate Talents, Capacities & Contributions of this Leadership Style have natural strengths that can be trained to make a great impact by:

- Elevating the quality of life for people.

- Nurturing the humanity of people so they can reach their potential.

- Seeking solutions that support the highest good for all.

- Creating opportunities for more people to see their own capacities.

- Discovering ways for more justice, fairness, and equity so everyone can thrive feeling their human rights are honored and safeguarded.

- Recognizing the inherent worth and value of each person so people can grow into the best version of themselves when great tools, environments, encouragement, support, and training are available.

The Vantage Points of people with this Leadership Style:

- They invest time to discover ways to uplift the quality of a process, system, or experience that activates the potential for people's innate nobility and dignity to be expressed.

- They strive to live, learn, work, create, collaborate, teach in environments that nourish their innate potential and inspire others through their example.

- They reflect on how people can begin to plant their "seeds of possibility" to take root and then grow into inspired acts of service.

- They create conditions for the growth and development of a flourishing, prosperous humanity.

- They are effective at supporting their own innate potential AND also contributing to the capacity-building and development of others to be their best selves.

A HERO'S STORY

I've had the amazing good fortune of having life experiences that put me in situations to meet people from a rich variety of cultures, communities, countries, and capacities that they incorporated in order to make their unique, positive impact in the world.

The person who was truly the epitome of embodying this Leadership Style of Humanity and Noble Actions is someone whom I've admired since the first day I met her. My admiration for her has organically, exponentially grown over the last 22 years. I still quote her and speak about her in presentations, in training sessions I facilitate, in my work with my clients, in my conversations with mentees, as well as with my close personal circle of friends. My husband has heard about her so much since he and I met, we both feel that she's with us and counseling us with her exquisite knowledge and worldly wisdom.

I always thought that if I were to be a contestant on a game show that allows me to "phone a friend", she would definitely be on the top of my list.

Since I was 20 years old and a full-time graduate student in Philadelphia, Ava was always a person who felt like a "lifeline" for me. When I was in the process of still unraveling my fears and trauma after the school shooting incident and had periods of insomnia, Ava created a sanctuary for me to recharge and reconnect with my courage.

The home she created with her incredible husband became one of my favorite places to spend my weekends. The surprising thing was that our weekends together revolved around service to the community, yet every part of it was bathed in light, laughter, and inspiration. She made everything flow with so much energy and enjoyment.

Ava and I first became close when she invited me to help with programs for young people that she designed as passion projects. Her sons were older and already living on their own in another state. Being an "empty nester", she provided a warm, maternal energy. She also became a powerful, trusted advisor and mentor to me.

She and her husband had been married for decades, yet they still went on dates and enjoyed each other's company immensely. They sat next to each other and held hands.
They were always thoughtful of what the other needed and they were very proactive in supporting each other's dreams come into reality. Their home was a true home of peace.

When people use the word "partnership", I instantly think of them as examples and role models.

For years, whenever I received Ava's invitation for a "work weekend session", I leapt at the chance to spend time with her. It never felt like work or a chore. Her list of actions always felt purposeful and balanced time for movies, music, delicious homemade snacks, meditating, admiring the sunset from their balcony that faced West, and conversations about the many exotic places she had lived in and the people who inspired her.

At the time, I hadn't lived outside the state of Pennsylvania, and it seemed incredible to see a person's passport that was filled with so many stamps.
From being born in Ethiopia, educated in India, graduated from a university in the United States, working in various countries in Africa and South America, and working in many states in the United States, she was an example of a world citizen. She loved and cared about people, and she felt a kinship with people from all different backgrounds and experiences.

I learned where countries were so I could picture where Ava would be traveling next. It felt just as exciting to hear her stories about the communities and companies that hired her for her wise counsel and facilitation skills. It blew my mind to realize that there are people who can travel the world and help companies become more ethical, more inclusive, more successful. She joked that her office was an airplane, and her desk was her oversized sofa.

Something that struck me then — and still strikes me now — was that there was always a clear passion reflected in her stories. Ava was passionate about young people developing their capacity to care about others, to have hope in their lives, and to connect deeply with the spiritual identity.

She would constantly remind young people to feel a kinship to heroes of the past who wanted to shatter the darkness of ignorance and create paths for humanity to become more fair, more respectful, more loving, and more humane towards each other.

Even when she was exhausted and very jetlagged, she was able to summon the energy and devotion to nurture the younger generations and convey that they are precious, valuable, and adored.
When I was in her presence, I always felt valuable and cared about. I felt seen and encouraged. Her advice always came from a mindful, reflective state.

One of the valuable gems of advice that she gave us during a weekend retreat at her home was about how service is meant to be joyful. In a very practical way, she explained that some things have to be done because it's the responsible thing to do.

However, her voice changed, and her posture became taller and steady. This was my cue to definitely pay close attention. I had seen this posture command the stages of large conferences and festivals. This was the posture that captivated audiences to pay attention in silence as she spoke, as well as sang songs that she led in unison.

It's an incredible thing to witness hundreds of strangers seated in an audience be moved to learn songs in a language they don't speak, yet feel enkindled by the profound sense of connection through the harmony of voices. I had seen this happen many times — simply by the way Ava exemplified the beauty that could be created when a sea of people was focused on the same thing.

Needless to say, I respected her voice immensely and her posture was a clue that something memorable was about to be shared.

Someone asked her how she's able to maintain so many types of service and support so many cultures in so many geographic places — often in other languages and in a variety of conditions that were sometimes quite modest and lacking comfort.

Her advice gave us all goosebumps and it was the catalyst of many creative ideas at that gathering: *"One of the most important things a person can spend time learning about is finding a path of service that brings your heart nothing but joy. Only joy. Because when you serve with a heart filled with joy, so many confirmations happen to support you and guide you."*

"What's your path of service that brings your heart nothing but joy, Ms. Ava?" one of my friends asked as a natural follow-up question.

She responded without hesitation or needing time to calculate her answer, *"Spending time mentoring young people like you. You're what brings my heart nothing but joy. Can't you tell?"*

Her eyes sparkled as she smiled at us, Intentionally looking at each of us who were sitting all around her living room.

As I'm typing these words to you, dear Reader, I have the same goosebumps as I had 22 years ago. Some people's impact on our lives is truly timeless and everlasting.

After years of serving together — and learning so much from her example — it was time for me to graduate, and I had some big decisions to make.

I told Ava about two of the job offers I received. The first was located in Philadelphia where I was currently living, and the other was in a small town in China that I didn't know if I was pronouncing correctly. After sharing all the details — the pros and cons, the challenges and the potential areas of growth, the practical and logistical, the emotional and financial — she thought for a moment to process the waterfall of information I had unleashed.

The pause continued and my heart started beating faster.

Ava was the first person I went to for her honest, thoughtful feedback and advice. She cared for me and had gotten to know me well. She understood some of the challenges I had been through and what I really cared about.

I wondered what she was going to say. I respected her opinion so much. She always encouraged me and liked me to go beyond my comfort zone, particularly with speaking and presenting at events. She knew I didn't like the spotlight and would rather fade into the background if it was my choice.

As I continued to wonder what she would say and what option she would encourage, she pondered in silence.

Then, her voice came:

"Hmm... You're doing such great things here in Philadelphia and there's momentum in what you're doing to help the young people with —"

Then she abruptly stopped mid-sentence. The pause was intentional. I got even more curious as to what her next thought would be.

"You know, Jaleh... This opportunity to move to China and work there... I think China would be good for you. Yes, I think having the experience in China would be good for you. I'd recommend China. I think you'd do well there and learn so many things that will help you in your life."

Boom. Ava had spoken. There was something validating in hearing her words. It was what my intuition was whispering, but was the opposite of my logical, practical side that favored staying-in-our-comfort-and-familiar-zone.

New score:

Intuition for Experiencing more Diversity: 2

versus Comfort and Familiar Zone: 1

Three months later, I had finished my internship and graduate school, I walked the stage to receive my diplomas, picked up my new passport without any stamps yet, and was on a plane to Shanghai to work in Zhenjiang, China — which would be my new home for the next 20 months.

A huge, continuous thanks to Ava and her great advice to invest in the possibilities that honor my values and development, no matter how unfamiliar or unclear the steps initially seemed.

My nearly two years in China provided me with experiences and connections that changed my life in every way, including improving my physical health and heart function, my next brilliant mentor who guided me throughout my time in Zhenjiang, a transformational trip across China with a group of Traditional Chinese Medicine physicians, overcoming another layer of trauma caused by the school shooting incident, learned another language, treated young children with a variety of health challenges, helped to facilitate a city-wide fundraiser to benefit the local orphanage, organized arts festivals to showcase the arts and music of East & West.

This period of service allowed me to create and enjoy wonderful bonds of friendship that still warm my heart. I found a community of friends in which I became a "little sister" (mei mei), an "auntie" (ai yi), and a teacher (lao shi). I found another place in the world that I felt a sense of home and joyful belonging. All of these blessings happened with people who didn't share the same nationality, native language, traditions, heritage, customs, or backgrounds as me. Yet, all of the layers of our mutual diversity became access point of connection, learning, understanding, expansion, and unity.

Not unity built on "sameness"; rather, unity built on a solid foundation of honoring each other's innate humanity and encouraging the expression of each other's nobility through acts of service.

IMPACT & INSIGHTS

After spending time with the amazing Ava — witnessing the bliss of the marriage of her and her beloved husband, traveling with them, cooking and enjoying foods from the many places they've lived together, listening to the eclectic CD collection they had acquired from artists from places they had visited, studying sacred books with them, making homemade candy and granola to give as gifts, mentoring high school students with them, facilitating workshops and helping to organize summer camp experiences for students, admiring how they make each other fall over with laughter because they adore each other's sense of humor — these ordinary and extraordinary experiences made me feel like my heart was flying.

I didn't know how much fun could be felt spending half of a Saturday running errands. One of the things that never felt particularly enjoyable in my life felt so different when I was with Ava.
She looked forward to being back home after weeks of traveling for work... just to buy her favorite grocery items at specific bakeries and shops for the hand-selected quality that she enjoyed.

One of my favorite parts was watching people's faces light up when she walked through the doors.
Even with a shorter stature, her presence was almost instantly felt. From the people stocking the shelves or at the cash register, from the owner of the shop or their younger workers... when Ava walked into their space, their eyes lit up.

They stopped what they were doing to greet her with a full smile that caused other people to smile, whether they knew her or not.

It was the closest thing I've felt to traveling with a rock star. Even when an actual famous actor who was shopping in the cereal aisle saw her, they struck up a conversation like they were old friends. She welcomed him to the city and wished him luck while filming his new project. He gave her a hug and said it was the first time he felt like he was spoken to like a regular person and not "talked at" like how many people interact with well-known people.

Ava actually invited him to help with a neighborhood party that she was helping to organize for some children, and he said if he would available, he'd be happy to help. Then he proceeded to give her his contact information and his wife's so they could stay in touch while they'd be in town for the 3 months of filming.

Then he thanked Ava for making his entire week and said he looked forward to the days in which more people made service approachable and cool like she did.

Even as I write this to you, dear Reader, years after this interaction happened, I remember the spark in both of their eyes - seeing each other through the lens of mutual respect, kindness, and encouragement.

They saw each other as connected drops of one ocean. They witnessed each other's humanity and value.

This was happening simultaneously with representing cross-sections of diversity with their exterior differences of skin color, gender, hair texture and style, nationality, ethnicity, native language, accent, stature, height (he was SO tall), as well as their experiences, professions, backgrounds, talents, skills, personalities, and so on.

What a gift to spend time with people who represent and embody the Leadership Style of Humanity and Noble Actions. It polished my vantage point to take notice of opportunities to express my own humanity and support others to express the fullness of their humanity… for everyone's highest good and deepest joy.

This vantage point may not always seem obvious and there are many messages and systems that try to take this Leadership Lens out of focus, yet these opportunities to uplift the human condition and quality of life of humanity are consistently present, nonetheless.

The power comes from exploring ways to train and sustain this much-needed capacity that benefits us all.

SOME WELL-KNOWN PEOPLE
WHO REPRESENT THIS LEADERSHIP STYLE

"In recognizing the humanity of our fellow beings,
we pay ourselves the highest tribute."
Thurgood Marshall,
Supreme Court Justice of the United States

*"Everywhere you turn, someone is trying to tear someone down
in some way; everywhere you go, there's a feeling of inadequacy,
or a feeling that you're not good enough.
I want to bring a certain light to the world."*
Alicia Keys,
Philanthropist, Grammy Award Winning Musician, Singer-Songwriter

*"I like bringing people together. I like making people who wouldn't
normally relate to one another find something in common through
live music experience for a genuine human exchange."*
"You have a limited time. Get to it. Embrace the imperfection."
Jon Batiste,
Academy Award & Grammy Award winning musician, Band Leader

*"Everybody has a talent — that if you look within — you can put
that talent to bring hope to others. We can all be part — not only
of feeding the world but believing in longer tables — not higher
walls Together, we can change the world. Some big problems have
simple solutions."*
Chef José Andrés,
Founder of World Central Kitchen

THE NUTRIENT THAT MIRRORS QUALITIES
OF THIS LEADERSHIP STYLE

This Leadership Style of Humanity and Noble Actions always reminds me of the nutrient Iron. Iron has so many positive effects for the body to function in healthy, balanced ways — both cellularly and on a systems level. It is essential to having sufficient energy and focus, regulation of temperature, digestion and gastrointestinal processes, the immune system's capacity to prevent illness, and the transport of oxygen to nourish all the cells of the body.

When there is a lack of sufficient iron, it creates a disruption in energy and leads to fatigue. People can also experience headaches, dizziness, shortness of breath, heart murmurs or other heart conditions, lowered cognitive performance such as memory or concentration.

Having people in our lives — personally and professionally — who represent the qualities of this Leadership Style can greatly uplift the energy of conversations, see beyond the current challenges, focus on inspiring goals, concentrate on the next milestone of a project, and the heartfelt desire to be part of the improvement of our communities and culture so that more people can experience fulfilling, thriving lives.

REFLECTION QUESTIONS TO PRACTICE
THIS LEADERSHIP QUALITY

1. Who inspires you with their acts of service that support the quality of life for humanity?

2. Reflect about an event that someone helped you — or someone else — feel seen, respected, and believed in?

3. How did you feel after receiving this gift — or by witnessing someone be cared about in an uplifting way — with each person's humanity respected and valued?

TREASURE HUNT INVITATION
TO TAKE INSPIRED ACTION

Within the next 24 hours — with what you already have access to — I invite you to decide to do an inspired act of service that brings your heart joy and supports the quality of life for another person (or people).

What impact will you be able to celebrate by doing this inspired act of service?

Bonus: After you complete this joyful act of service, reflect on what your favorite part was. You can journal, draw, sketch, paint, make a voice note, write about it in any format you wish.

6

THE LEADERSHIP STYLE OF ELEVATING EXPERIENCES & MEMORY-MAKING

Joy gives us wings! In times of joy our strength is more vital, our intellect keener, and our understanding less clouded. We seem better able to cope with the world and to find our sphere of usefulness.

'Abdu'l-Bahá

I believe that without memories there is no life, and that our memories should be of happy times.

unknown

One of the best ways to make yourself happy in the present is to recall happy times from the past. Photos are a great memory-prompt, and because we tend to take photos of happy occasions, they weight our memories to the good.

Gretchen Rubin

You shouldn't wait for other people to make special things happen. You have to create your own memories.

Heidi Klum

"A life-long blessing for children is to fill them with warm memories of times together. Happy memories become treasures in the heart to pull out on the tough days of adulthood."

Charlotte Kasl

A SPECIAL PLACE IN THE WORLD
THAT INSPIRED THIS CHAPTER

One of favorite cafes in northern Portugal in a small town outside of Porto called Penafiel.

It's a beautiful, cozy, corner cafe that serves all types of Portuguese pastries, teas, and coffees. I always marvel at the intricate tilework on the walls - from floor to ceiling.

The staff who work there always greet me with warm smiles and always seem to understand my less-than-perfect Portuguese, which is such a relief as a foreigner living in a new country.

NICKNAME FOR THIS LEADERSHIP STYLE:
PATII MAKERS

In 2013, I had a client who is a wonderful representative of this Leadership Style of Elevating Experiences and Memory-Making.

I started calling her **"Path Maker"** because of her remarkable ability to ascertain how to infuse meaningful details into processes, strategies, and experiences that cultivate more joyful memories. Over the years, I've noticed that all of my clients with this leadership style have an uncanny ability to contribute to a culture that has more consistent bright spots and highlight reels.

DEDICATED TO

"Annie"

BELIEFS, VALUES, VANTAGE POINTS,
AND UNIQUE QUALITIES OF THIS LEADERSHIP TEAM

The essence of this Leadership Style of Elevating Experiences and Memory-Making lies in fulfilling two fundamental needs: keen observation of the current state of experiences and processes, whether in professional, personal, social, or creative spheres, and a deep-rooted desire to enhance the quality of those experiences.

Leaders embodying this style view the world through a unique lens— one that seeks to improve the richness of people's encounters. They possess a genuine care for creating wonderful memories and ensuring that individuals feel truly alive in their lives. Their own yearning for moments that transcend the ordinary fuels their dedication to crafting experiences that ignite joy and awaken all the senses.
They possess an acute ability to recognize and appreciate the subtle beauty within each encounter, constantly striving to refine and enhance the quality of experiences.

They understand the profound impact that extraordinary experiences have on the formation of memories.

These cherished memories become the highlight reel of one's life—a collection of standout moments that define a week, a month, a holiday, or even an entire lifetime. Their aspiration is for people to look back and feel a sense of fulfillment, knowing that they have lived well.

The emphasis here is not on extravagant or costly experiences, but on the meaningful. These leaders deeply value the importance of imbuing experiences with significance. They yearn to elevate ordinary days, ensuring that life does not pass by without a tapestry of meaningful, delicious, and vibrant moments. Beautiful experiences give rise to beautiful memories.

The Innate Talents, Capacities & Contributions to Focus On:
Natural Strengths that can be trained and make a significant impact...

- Elevates the quality of life for people to feel alive and aligned with their lives

- Care about the quality of memories and experiences that nourish their lives

- Desire people to have a life worth living and to use their time well.

- Activates individual's quest for aligned paths, where adventure, stories, fun, deep sense of joy can be experienced

- Seeking highest quality of life for all people

- Creates opportunities for more people to see their capacities and feel them develop

- Discovers potential for more wisdom so everyone can thrive feeling their humanity is nourished and strong

- Capable of seeing the inherent worth and value of every child can grow into the best version of themselves when great tools, environment, encouragement, support, and training are available.

Vantage Points and Points of Curiosity:

- How it can be possible to uplift the quality of a process, system, or experience

- Where is the Potential for people to live, learn, work, create, collaborate in environments that nourish them

- How can people begin to plant their "seeds of potential" to take root and to grow and flourish

- Can help people see the possibilities and potential in their own capacity-building and development

What's obvious to them but can often be other people's blind or foggy spots because they can shift from a big picture goal to the details necessary to begin making progress towards that objective.

Imagine the benefit to your life, your team, your community, your organization with contributions of people who can:

- See big picture possibilities and envision the goals, and then zoom into the details that support the goal

- Focus on the big picture view that allows people to derive more energy, joy, and inspiration

- Communicate their perspectives in a way that naturally fuels the energy & discernment with collaborating and decision-making

- Focus on seeing the expansive vision of possibilities that may seem obvious or easily apparent to them, yet oftentimes goes overlooked by the majority of people who are feeling the stress, frustration, or pressure of the challenging circumstance.

- See the milestones and steps that are meaningful to make the goal into a reality

- Maintain focus on the points of the process that activate a higher degree of passion, purpose, or clarity among the team and the people who are impacted by the project or service.

- Make progress an enjoying enterprise

- Communicate stories about possible paths that lead to more progress, adventure, and joy

CONTRIBUTIONS TO COMMUNITIES AND CULTURES

Their motto: *"When it's light, it's right."*

This Leadership Style develops people who can help create - or refine - the processes that make the vision able to come into reality and be felt in tangible ways.

They help people's ideas progress and not get blocked by feeling bored, fatigue, frustration.

They are dedicated to making progress and achievements an enjoying enterprise

They enjoy creating or refining experiences that are memorable, meaningful, and multi-sensory

How they show up:

- They have a large & capable vantage point to see how the meaningful details initiate a catalyst that creates a ripple effect towards the big picture of possibilities.

- They notice unrealized PATHS and PROCESSES that could make a significant difference to making greater progress and transformation - not only quantitatively but also qualitatively

- They believe that progress scales faster when more people are nourished and activated by uplifting experiences, which enables them to be more willing and capable of contributing their talents

- They make progress an enjoyable enterprise for the people involved in the work

A HERO'S STORY

One of my favorite humans in my life is a person who always made me feel so happy, in the very instant I saw her. Her name is Annie and she continues to be an inspiration to me about how to enjoy as much sweetness and create a life that we love and adore. Watching her and her husband interact gave me an real-life example of how magical some partnerships are when both people show up for each other. They both joyfully enhanced each other's well-being, and they seemed to truly enjoy building a bright, beautiful life together.

Since I was a child, every time we saw each other, she gave me the biggest, warmest hugs and said how happy she was to see me.
As a teenage, she invited me to enjoy lip sync performances, karaoke and dance parties, and talent shows to .

As a college student, she often sent me surprise "good luck" cards in the mail before exams to remind me that the entire university experience is multi-faceted and there to be savored. I loved receiving her emails with jokes and stories of our fun adventures together. Every message was special because it was from her - even if it was only 3 sentences. She always helped me see life as a gift that's filled with possibilities to explore, to open new doors, to dare to try new experiences that brought more laughter and joy to my heart.

I saved - and even printed out - every message from her.

Every experience and interaction with her elevated my mood, my mind, and my memories. Her name is Annie.

At group events, I always ran around people to get a seat next to hers. Just sitting close to her made me feel so happy and it didn't matter what the program was about. We giggled together, shared stories, updated each other about life, giggled more, danced together in our chairs, and then she would give me some of the most heartfelt, wise advice.

Annie infused into every space an encouraging reminder to not wait until the end result is achieved, but to also design the path with steps that progress towards the "finish line" and that doesn't drain people's energy.

Instead, the process should nourish people's energy, creativity, and learning so that progress and the achieved goals can be celebrated by all who contributed.

IMPACT & INSIGHTS

Simply being in her company made my heart feel lighter and also braver to believe that I could venture outside my comfort zone and experience more of the world. Thanks to her, I accepted invitations to work in countries outside of the United States and be excited for the opportunities that helped me be nourished by cultures, friends, colleagues, projects, and organizations that I hadn't experienced in my home cities and state. Instead of being afraid of all the unknowns, I trusted myself and found trustworthy people to collaborate with well so we could contribute to the people we served. The way Annie embodied her Leadership Style gave me permission to have fun in the process.

When I was living in China in the early 2000's, I had the great opportunity to work with the Foreign Affairs Office who encouraged me to serve the community. With a degree in Physical Therapy, I gravitated to working with children with special needs. I also saw how much the arts was so deeply valued in Chinese culture.

So, when the idea of organizing a fundraiser to support the medical care for children who lived at the local welfare center came to mind, I thought of Annie and reflected on the question, "How would Annie do this?" Then the idea struck loudly and clearly.

Let's make the fundraiser feel like a huge celebration of the arts, the culture, the talents of local Chinese students and professionals alike. Let's shine a spotlight on how much beauty there is when people come together to enjoy traditional musical instruments, dance, fashion, paintings, calligraphy, and singers. Let's give people a memorable event that bridges East and West, and gives them the opportunity to support a worthy cause at the same time.

Annie's example was a guiding light. People heard about my idea and showed up fully to participate and make it a success. The target goal for the monetary amount was surpassed beyond my initial vision, which was incredibly exciting. We could support the surgeries for many young children who could then have a healthier body for the rest of their lives, and they could also have a higher probability of being adopted.

Surprisingly, I don't remember the amount of money we raised, but I do remember the conversations of the team who helped plan the fundraiser. I do remember that I was drinking a jasmine tea and took notes on a napkin during the initial conversation that started the process. I do remember the dress rehearsal when all the team members were focusing on their role and being incredibly helpful to each other.

I do remember the spotlight on our two emcees for the evening - one local lady from Zhenjiang and one young man from the United States. I remember the audience clapping so loudly when the American spoke Mandarin and the Chinese lady spoke English so everyone would understand what was being said.

I remember the huge smile of the student who was the winner of the raffle grand prize. I remember the elderly couple who won one of the calligraphy pieces that was offered by an award-winning student from Zhenjiang.

I remember the audience clapping along to the music of the fashion show that showcased pieces from a local boutique owner.

I remember being most nervous about walking on the stage because I was "volunteered" to participate in the fashion show, even though I tried to make any excuse I could think of in order to avoid the spotlight.

I remember feeling alive. I remember feeling that a small team created this magical event that was bringing so much joy to people behind the stage, on the stage, and in the audience.

I remember the team hugging and deciding to go for dumplings at the local Night Market because we were so hungry and needed to have a place to reflect on what we just created together.

I remember feeling like I was exactly in the right place, at the right time, doing exactly the right thing. It was my first time organizing an event in another country, and I felt so connected and supported.

As I'm typing these words, I'm re-living every detail. I'm marinading in the loving, generous tone of the event.

I'm feeling grateful that I was able to be part of something that connected and unified so many people from 14 countries. I'm feeling more appreciation for my life and the time I've been gifted. Undoubtedly, this experience is part of my life's highlight reel.

Annie's example has helped me remember that we cannot control everything, and anything we can design or adjust can set us up to have a more uplifting, joyful tone in how we show up each day. This greatly impacts how we feel, what we think, what we do, who we spend time with, and where we live our lives. People, places, and experiences are essential elements of a well-lived life, and they are the building blocks for a life filled with memories that we can revisit, reinforce, and share with others.

SOME WELL-KNOWN PEOPLE WHO REPRESENT THIS LEADERSHIP STYLE

*"Be healthy and take care of yourself, but be happy
with the beautiful things that make you, you.
If everything was perfect, you would never learn,
and you would never grow.
I embrace mistakes. They make you who you are.
Never let success go to your head,
never let failure get to your heart."*
Beyonce

*"We all have our time machines. Some take us back, they're called
memories. Some take us forward, they're called dreams."*
Jeremy Irons

"Adventure is important in life. Making memories matters…
Effort from imagination and following adventure creates stories
that you keep forever. And anyone can do it."
Rob Lowe

"We didn't realize we were making memories,
we just knew we were having fun."
A.A. Milne

"Does it spark joy?"
Marie Kondo

"It's realizing that a great dream is not as good as a great memory.
The dream can be had by anyone. The memory – must be made."
Eric Thomas

A NUTRIENT THAT MIRRORS QUALITIES
OF THIS LEADERSHIP STYLE

When I work with clients with this Leadership Style, I often see how they impact the people in their sphere of influence similarly to the way magnesium supports the human body.

The Benefits of Magnesium are significant. It is needed to make DNA, protein, and bone tissue. It's important for muscles and nerves to work properly, which are essential for healthy movement, strength, flexibility, and stamina. Magnesium also helps keep blood sugar and blood pressure at the right levels, which are also necessary for a body to move and perform well.

A body with difficulty moving has challenges in every other physiological system, such as respiration, digestion, and circulation. Another benefit to magnesium is that it may also reduce stress and improve symptoms of anxiety and depression, such as headaches and difficulty sleeping.

When individuals and groups of people can imagine what's possible, plan with clarity, and move with enthusiasm and consistent action, they tend to make greater gains and see improvements over time. They also tend to learn from setbacks and progress, incorporate joy and fun whenever possible, and they decide to continue progressing forward until they achieve their goals.

These are some of the improvements that this Leadership Style are committed to, which leads to a stronger, more resilient, and more magnetic community and culture.

REFLECTION QUESTIONS TO PRACTICE
THIS LEADERSHIP QUALITY

1. **What is one of my favorite memories that make me feel joy, happiness, connection, or hope?**

2. **What made that experience meaningful and important for you?**

TREASURE HUNT INVITATION TO TAKE
INSPIRED ACTION"

- Take a moment and think about how you could create a positive, joyful memory **today** for yourself.

- Put your plan into action and try it out. It doesn't have to be perfect.

- See how it sets up your day to feel brighter and live in more color.

- Next, reflect on ways you could include at least one other person to experience more joy and have a sweet memory for themselves.

You can think to yourself:

How can I take a "regular" day and create an experience that infuses a joyful surprise for us to have a memory worth having - to make today count - or to have today in our "highlight reel" of the month or year?

7

THE LEADERSHIP STYLE OF RELATIONSHIP & COMMUNITY-BUILDING

We are neurobiologically hard-wired for
connection with each other. In the absence of
connection, there is always suffering. We need
language to forge connection.

Brene Brown

A SPECIAL PLACE IN THE WORLD
THAT INSPIRED THIS CHAPTER

I'm starting this chapter while sitting in one of my favorite writing places - a bookstore.

It's not just any bookstore. It's in my hometown of Harrisburg, Pennsylvania. It's the bookstore that I spent lots of time reading, having uplifting conversations, and outlining creative ideas.

It's the spot that I starting imagining what this book could be, how I could organize it, and what stories I might include.

It's called The Midtown Scolar Bookstore in Harrisburg, Pennsylvania. It's a two-story building that's surrounded by books on any topic I could imagine, and it builds community. They feature and spotlight authors, musicians, poets, and artists - both local and from around the country. I appreciate how they're creating a sense of community and support for artists who are contributing their talents to share ideas, knowledge, and insights from their lived experiences.

NICKNAME FOR THIS LEADERSHIP STYLE:
BOND MAKERS

There's a client that I had from a well-known company who is a shining example of this Leadership Style of Relationship and Community-Building. His dedication to supporting the building of strong, reliable relationships in his team was such an example of a bond-maker that I started calling him Mr. Bond, which he enjoyed very much.

DEDICATED TO

"Aaron"

BELIEFS, VALUES, VANTAGE POINTS, AND UNIQUE
QUALITIES OF THIS LEADERSHIP TEAM

**Creating bonds between people and growing a strong community
is no easy feat.**

**Humans are complex as individuals and it can take time to create a
good relationship with oneself, let along creating lasting, healthy,
strong connections between people who are related, have things
in common, or belong to the same group or community.**

**The process of developing close, interpersonal relationships
between two or more people who don't know each other or who
represent groups that haven't yet had sufficient time to interact
and understand each other can pose additional challenges.**

**This is where the Leadership Style of Relationship and Community-
Building shine.**

The leadership style focused on relationship and community building
is one of the rarer styles, but it holds immense value. It is a highly
nuanced and detail-oriented approach to leadership.

Leaders who embrace this style deeply care about fostering strong
bonds, understanding the dynamics between individuals, and
nurturing healthy relationships.

They believe that the quality of relationships within a community or organization is fundamental to its success, even surpassing technological advancements and available resources. From their perspective, thriving cultures, societies, and ecosystems are built upon strong relationships.

These leaders are dedicated to enhancing and improving the quality of connections between individuals. They recognize that when the relationship between an individual and themselves is healthy and robust, it sets the stage for healthier and stronger external relationships with others. They hold a firm belief that individuals have unique gifts to offer and can contribute most effectively when surrounded by a supportive and nurturing community. Community-building is a reciprocal process where individuals benefit while also actively contributing.

However, when practiced within a community or culture, it benefits everyone. Identifying individuals with this style can be observed through their inclination to address breakdowns and misunderstandings in relationships. They actively engage in mediating and facilitating quality conversations to repair damaged bonds. Instead of avoiding problems, they face them head-on, bringing practical solutions and identifying the root causes of challenges.

These leaders act as first responders, offering hope and opportunities for collaboration. Their approach to problem-solving involves seeking practical solutions rather than merely complaining. They are committed to the long-term process of building thriving communities and work tirelessly to create conditions for cooperation and unity.

They understand the intricate and complexities nature of human relationships and dynamics, and they play a unifying role within their family, group, community, or company.

CONTRIBUTIONS TO COMMUNITIES AND CULTURES

This Leadership Style's Vantage Point and Values:

- Seek to improving the Quality of Relationships & Connection between people

- Deep care for people to have reliable support to learn, collaborate, and create desired results

- Dedicated to help (themselves and other people) not feel alone or isolated in challenging situations

- Yearn to have such strong bonds between people that there is support during challenges and support during celebration times

- Want to close the gaps that divides or isolates people from one another, that can weaken the bonds between people, that weakens the fabric of a healthy & thriving community

- Create opportunities to connect people so they can feel safe to get to know each other in genuine ways

- See connection and bonds between people as a necessary element for a productive, successful, meaningful life that feels fulfilling and impactful

- Contribute to a society that allows more people to feel a sense of belonging and raise generations of people who can add to the well-being of any community and uplevel each other's quality of life

A HERO'S STORY

One of the most wealthy clients I ever worked with was quite early in my career when I was in my early 30's and he was in his 80's. We'll call him Aaron.

Aaron had every financial comfort and never worried about being able to afford any physical product. A few years before meeting him, he sustained a bad fall while walking to his mailbox at the end of his long driveway, resulting in a fractured hip that required surgery.

While in his hospital room, he had a roommate who was also a gentleman in his 80's, yet the two men had some differences. Aaron's roommate had a steady stream of visitors every day - his wife, his children, his grandchildren, his nieces, his neighbors, his friends. All day long, the hospital room was like a subway station with visitors coming in and out of the doorway to see their loved one and surround him with love during his hospital stay.

While Aaron watched his roommate be surrounded by loved ones who cared so deeply about him, he realized that he wasn't leading his life in the same way. In three days in the hospital, Aaron only had one visitor - his personal assistant who came to look after some of the logistical details and make sure he was comfortable.

It was in that hospital room that Aaron decided to make some changes that would nourish an unmet need that he realized was truly important. He wanted to prioritize connections and relationships so he could feel proud about the legacy he was leaving behind.

Up until that point in his life, Aaron focused on professional success and was excellent in his business. He was indeed wealthy, but he told me that he had often felt lonely because he never prioritized relationships nor did he create a community of genuine friends, colleagues, and confidants.

As he told me about his story, I could see that there was genuine sadness and regret…which was devastating.

After he recovered from his hip surgery, he decided to invest more of his time and energy into building connections and reconnecting with people who he respected and cared about. This became his focus, and he excelled in making his vision a reality.

IMPACT & INSIGHTS

Three years later, we met at a conference that we were both speakers, and he had mentees there from his company, as well as two family members who started working with him on a social justice project. Another older lady was sitting next to him, and I naturally wondered who she was because of the way Aaron responded to her. Every time she spoke, his attention was completed drawn to her and she had a way of making him smile and laugh.

Aaron had reconnected with his older sister, who had been a close confidant to him when they were growing up. Somehow over the years, he drifted away from her and didn't make plans to spend much time with her and her children. He told me that this one of his greatest regrets because "Big Sis" was like a second mother to him and always made him feel valued and loved.

So when Aaron decided to prioritize quality time with loved ones and rebuild relationships, she was the first person he called. As a sister who has a brother, I felt happy for them and relieved that their bond had never been broken, although it needed to be nourished and tended to again.

Aaron was surrounded by people who valued him, respected him, and were proud to be connected. He looked so happy and light. The next day of the conference, he told me that his focus was to be an example of how much richer life is when we work with excellence in our professional lives and always remember how dynamic life is so we need each other.

We need to be connected to people who care about us.

I'll never forget the next thing he told me. It feels like it was only weeks ago instead of years ago:
"Jaleh, promise this old man that you'll lead your life like love is your oxygen, and true relationships are your fuel."

I will forever hold Aaron in high regard, remember his example, and practice it in the best way I can. What a great way to lead our lives. Thank you Aaron.

SOME WELL-KNOWN PEOPLE WHO REPRESENT
THIS LEADERSHIP STYLE

*"You cannot get through a single day without having
an impact on the world around you.
What you do makes a difference, and you have to decide
what kind of difference you want to make."*
Jane Goodall

A NUTRIENT THAT MIRRORS QUALITIES
OF THIS LEADERSHIP STYLE

Clients that I've worked with throughout the years have consistently said that healthy human connections and relationships are like the oxygen in life. So I liken this Leadership Style with B12 because it's a nutrient that helps to build healthy DNA and helps nerve and blood cells function well. It prevents blood conditions that cause fatigue and weakness, and it's important for the distribution of oxygen.

In the human body, red blood cells transport oxygen to all our cells, tissues, and organs.

Any cell that doesn't receive a sufficient amount of oxygen begins to lose its strength and cannot function well. A weak system leads to a difficulty moving, walking, thinking, problem-solving having energy to do tasks, digest food, and maintain balance.

Just as we all need B12 to have a healthy body, any community, organization, and culture needs healthy relationships and connections between people in order to be successful throughout generations.

REFLECTION QUESTIONS TO PRACTICE THIS LEADERSHIP QUALITY

How would you like to feel in your closest relationships?

1. What qualities do you want to be consistently present in your closest 5 relationships?

2. What qualities can you bring into your relationships that nourish them to be reciprocally beneficial?

TREASURE HUNT INVITATION TO TAKE INSPIRED ACTION

1. Think of a person who has wonderful relationships and community. A. What's a quality you admire in how this person shows up for the people in their life, their team, their family, or their community? B. What's one thing you can do this week to nourish one of the relationships in your life - either with your family, friends, partner, team member, colleague, neighbor, etc?

2. After you take action, reflect on how the experience went and how you can continue to build healthy, respectful relationships in your life. You can journal about it, have a conversation about it, make a video about it, or sketch out ideas in your favorite app.

8

THE LEADERSHIP STYLE OF SENSIBILITY & EMPATHY

The highest form of knowledge is empathy, for it requires us to suspend our egos and live in another's world.

Plato

A SPECIAL PLACE IN THE WORLD
THAT INSPIRED THIS CHAPTER

There's a cafe outside of Porto, Portugal that is right by the water and has a wonderful view of a lighthouse. I always enjoy this spot because there's a panoramic view of the Atlantic Ocean in front of me and a still-working lighthouse to my right. Eight beams light, rotating clockwise, rhythmically and consistently providing a strong focal point for all the ships that are moving along their journey, out at sea.

It's so reassuring to know that no matter how choppy and stormy the ocean can get, there's a steady point to look up and notice where land is, where home is, where safety is.

NICKNAME FOR THIS LEADERSHIP STYLE:
LIGHTHOUSE

When moving through an emotional storm, we can get thrown off our game, lose our sense of balance, get filled with doubt and uncertainty.

Years ago, I had the honor of working with an extraordinary leader and she quickly became one of my most memorable clients. One of these reasons was because of how she provided a sense of calm, steadiness, and resolve to everyone in her company.

No matter what the challenge or difficulty was, regardless of the high level of intensity that was necessary to get her team through the stormy situation, she commanded the ship and successfully led the team safely to shore.

So, after calculating her Leadership Style, I started calling her The Lighthouse. The nickname stuck and her inner circle team still affectionately refer to her by this title.

DEDICATED TO

Angel

BELIEFS, VALUES, VANTAGE POINTS, AND UNIQUE QUALITIES OF THIS LEADERSHIP TEAM

Many people are caring individuals and have the ability to practice emotional intelligence or emotional awareness.

People who have this Leadership Style and have developed it in their lives tend to have a complex, unique, highly attuned capacity for sensing the emotional state of themselves and of others.

In general, people care about themselves and other people. They have a certain innate amount of capacity to show compassion towards people. They can use their unique capacity to cultivate and contribute to the individual & collection state of emotional well-being.

This Leadership Style team - represented by people born all around the world and regardless of their profession, education, culture, nationality, generation, or age - have shown a much greater "gallon-measure" capacity to sense, perceive, attune, and gain awareness of what is the "emotional temperature" in a particular situation, environment, or gathering.

CONTRIBUTIONS TO COMMUNITIES AND CULTURES

In the realm of leadership and service, there exists a rare and extraordinary style that can be found in the final chapter of our exploration. It is the style of sensibility and empathy, a combination that holds immense value and significance.

Sensibility, in this context, refers to the ability to appreciate and respond to complex emotional influences. It goes beyond mere logical analysis, encompassing a heightened awareness and understanding of emotions through the senses.

However, it should be noted that sensibility does not imply being overly emotional or easily upset.

Empathy, on the other hand, is the capacity to understand and share the feelings of others, even when they are in different circumstances or living through diverse experiences.

This leadership style of sensibility and empathy is represented by only 7% of all leadership styles examined in my research over the past two decades.

Remarkably, individuals embodying this style can be found across genders, cultures, nationalities, educational backgrounds, professions, and interests. This leadership style is not contingent on external factors or personality traits but encompasses a diverse range of people, including both young and old.

Those who possess this style possess a remarkable ability to profoundly impact the emotional well-being of those they interact with. As they cultivate trusted relationships, gain knowledge, and foster healthy connections, they develop a deep sense of self-trust and emotional resilience. Crucially, they experience the transformative power of at least one nourishing and respectful relationship, whether it be with a parent, sibling, or friend. In such relationships, their high degree of empathy is embraced rather than seen as a flaw, enabling them to reach extraordinary levels of emotional well-being.

The effects of their presence extend far and wide, benefitting not only strangers but also friends, community members, family, and loved ones. People often express a sense of safety and comfort in their company, feeling free to be themselves and share their thoughts without fear of judgment.

Even without explicitly offering advice or therapeutic interventions, their mere presence, demeanor, and body language have a remarkable ability to lighten the emotional burden of others.

The environment is infused with a sense of collective well-being, fostering emotional equilibrium and enabling individuals to process their emotions with greater clarity and self-reflection.

This leadership style has a profound impact on fostering empathy and sensibility in others. People learn to approach their own challenges in a healthier and more productive manner, avoiding damaging triggers and negative ripple effects. By embracing a wide spectrum of emotions and recognizing that they do not define our value or character, this style of leadership encourages individuals to navigate difficulties and challenging situations with resilience and grace.

In essence, this style serves as a poignant reminder that emotions are part of the human experience. We all feel pain, fear, disappointment, joy, excitement, and grief along the vast spectrum of human emotions. Emotions come and go like waves, but they do not define who we are at our core. By creating a space where emotions can be felt and processed without devastating our character, these leaders inspire us to face challenges head-on, even when situations become incredibly difficult.

At the end of the day, emotions are like waves, while the human spirit is designed to be resilient. It's not necessary to suppress or numb our emotions, but we also don't have to let them dictate how we speak or treat others.

Those who embody this leadership style create environments where people can fully experience their feelings while navigating them in a healthy and respectful manner. They understand that belittling or disrespecting others is not what people need when they are in an unsteady emotional state. Instead, they strive to cultivate spaces where individuals can process their emotions without compromising their self-respect or potential for growth.

This unique leadership style emphasizes the importance of consciousness being in the driver's seat, rather than being triggered by emotions. When someone is triggered, their language and behavior tend to differ from when they are in a calm and thoughtful state. Leaders of this style are incredibly supportive, patient, and intuitive, sensing when someone is going through something even without being told directly.

A HERO'S STORY

I had a transformative encounter with a five-year-old who embodied this leadership style brilliantly, becoming my unexpected hero. It happened on a day when I was feeling utterly devastated after attending a funeral for my best friend, who passed away suddenly at the age of 22. Seeking solace, I took a walk in my parents' neighborhood and walked around my usual "thinking place" where I had shared countless conversations and fun moments with my late friend.

In this park, I encountered a little girl playing with her older sisters, under the watchful eye of her grandmother. To my surprise, the smallest child approached me as though we were old friends, even though we had never met. Her innocent brown eyes met mine, and I couldn't help but take a deep breath, feeling a glimmer of relief as the tension around my heart began to dissipate. She reached out her tiny hand, painted with pink nail polish, in a gesture of friendship. I hesitated, concerned about her grandmother's reaction to a stranger being so close to her precious grandchild.

I looked at her grandmother and greeted her politely, but the little girl persisted, extending her arm as high as she could and gently patting my knee, all while clutching her stuffed puppy. In a sweet, lullaby-like voice, she reassured me, saying, *"It's okay. Don't be sad. Everything will be alright."*

The gut-wrenching tension within me continued to melt away as she hugged my leg and shared her profound wisdom. She acknowledged that she, too, experienced sadness but assured me that it would get better. She invited me to play with her and her puppy, promising that it would bring joy and alleviate my pain. Her perceptiveness and kindness touched me deeply. Throughout the day, adults had offered various phrases and advice to help me through my grief, but none of it had resonated. Yet, this little angel, a stranger to me, spoke to my heart in a way that no one else could.

In that moment, I marveled at the power of her presence. How could someone I had never met, who had left her sisters mid-play, have such a profound impact on me? Her grandmother, initially concerned about our interaction, realized the depth of her granddaughter's compassion and care. She said, "You're sad. I want your heart to smile again."

As we exchanged glances, I struggled to hold back tears, overwhelmed by the genuine love and concern radiating from this child. With her, I felt truly seen and cared for, and my sadness took a brief respite. I was in awe of her extraordinary capacity for compassion, thoughtfulness, and encouragement. In that moment, she shared her leadership gifts with me, precisely when I needed them the most.

IMPACT & INSIGHTS

This life-changing encounter occurred in the summer of 2001, yet the memory of the entire interaction remains vivid in my mind until today.

I can still remember the pink butterfly barrettes in her beautifully braided hair. I can still remember the warmth of her hand as she patted my knee and gave my leg a full-body hug.

Then she said something so sweet and reassuring.
"Are you okay now?"
And I responded with less constriction around my heart and throat, *"Yeah, Angel. I'm better now. Thanks to you."*

She smiled at me with her face glowing with the hot August afternoon sun. She waved goodbye and said, *"Bye bye, new friend. See you soon."*

I see her in my mind all the time. Although she's now in her 20's and a full adult, I will always remember how brilliant of a leader she already was as a young child. She taught me by her example that emotions can be felt and are part of life, and that there are lighthouses stationed at points to anchor us and remind us that the emotional storm can pass and we can come back to a sense of steadiness. We just have to be patient and show ourselves - and others - grace in our vulnerability, in our suffering, and in our humanity.

Sometimes - like in August 2001 - I needed a lighthouse; I needed Angel. Sometimes I can be serve as a lighthouse for myself and replay Angels advice and gems of truth spoken in her cute, chipmunk-like voice.

There will be moments when we all need a lighthouse, and there will be moments when we can serve as a lighthouse for someone else. Both are ok. Both are valuable.
Both are part of being a service-driven leader.

Just like the little angel who brightened my day, these reminders exist to show us that no matter how overwhelming or despairing a situation may seem, we are not alone in our experiences.
Our feelings are valid, and we have the capacity to rediscover joy and unity, to regain our confidence and navigate the challenges that life presents.

I am immensely grateful for this leadership style because it can be daunting to feel deeply and to empathize with the emotions of others. Yet, it offers a thoughtful and nourishing alternative—an ecosystem where we can thrive, not in despair but in hope, not in grief but in joy, fostering creativity and growth.

These leaders serve as beautiful reminders that we have the resilience to overcome difficult circumstances and emerge even stronger, more capable, and empathetic.

They teach us patience and self-compassion.

I hold great admiration for this leadership style, and seek out ways to develop strong connections with people who are engaged with developing these leadership qualities.

For instance, when I was walking through the park, consumed by numbness and lacking any hope of a smile, little Angel appeared. Rather than telling me to smile, she effortlessly did something that brought a genuine smile to my face. Her actions became a turning point in my grieving process, and her strength, wisdom, and beauty radiated through her young self, bringing light back into my heart.

SOME WELL-KNOWN PEOPLE WHO REPRESENT THIS LEADERSHIP STYLE

"There is a nobility in compassion, a beauty in empathy..."
John Connolly

"Empathy is seeing with the eyes of another, listening with the ears of another and feeling with the heart of another."
Alfred Adler.

"You can only understand people if you feel them in yourself."
John Steinbeck

"If you judge people, you have no time to love them."
Mother Teresa.

A NUTRIENT THAT MIRRORS QUALITIES OF THIS LEADERSHIP STYLE

Vitamin E is the nutrient that reminds me most of the qualities and contributions of the Leadership Style of Empathy and Sensibility.

Vitamin E helps maintain healthy skin and eyes, as well as strengthens the body's immune system, which is a defense system against illness and infection. I liken the qualities of Vitamin E to that of a warrior's armour and shield before going into battle.

Many necessary layers of protection are offered to us by healthy skin and good vision. Although our eyes and skin can seem quite vulnerable and not the "toughest" tissues we have in our bodies, they are incredibly important, resilient, and preserve the integrity of some of our most important senses and internal systems.

The emotional well-being of a team, community, organization, or company are also incredibly important for the desired success and impact. So, it's essential to activate, encourage, and develop the nourishing qualities of this Leadership Style in your sphere of influence - aka the Vitamin E - in order to experience the best possible results.

REFLECTION QUESTIONS TO PRACTICE
THIS LEADERSHIP QUALITY

"How am I feeling in this moment?"

"What would help me feel more steady, more in tune, more hopeful, more connected?"

"What action can I do today that would act like a pebble that would be a catalyst or create a ripple effect for more emotional steadiness and well-being?"

TREASURE HUNT INVITATION TO TAKE
INSPIRED ACTION

Pause for a moment and reflect on a challenging time when you felt unsure, sad, confused, disappointed, or overwhelmed.

Think of someone who showed up to accompany you during that challenging day or moment.

Did they sit with you, have a nice chat, treat you for a snack or meal, go for a walk together, offer a reassuring hug or words that brought comfort? (These are just a few examples.)
Much like Angel did for me, your invitation is to be ready to accompany someone in need this week.

Plan to spend time with someone who may be having a tough day or going through a difficult situation - and could use a positive interaction. Ask them if you can take them out for coffee, visit them, bring them food, or simply take a walk together. You can even send them an encouraging message via text or make a little video for them.

Remind them of their importance, offer a reassuring word, share a funny or light-hearted story, share something personal that reminds them that they're not alone in life. Accompany them through their challenging moment - in the best way you know how.

Perfection is not the goal. Showing up as yourself is enough.

After practicing a quality of this Leadership Style, observe how you feel about the act of service you offered.

Appreciate the fact that you noticed an opportunity to show up for someone in a time of need. You might have been an unexpected hero or angel of the day.

Years later, they may still remember this gesture you gave - just as I often do with Angel.

9

THE LEADERSHIP STYLE OF TRUTH & TRUST

Trust life, and it will teach you, in joy and sorrow,
all you need to know.

James Baldwin

A SPECIAL PLACE IN THE WORLD
THAT INSPIRED THIS CHAPTER

I'm writing this chapter from a place new to me. It's the first time I'm standing in this town of Ericeira, Portugal.

I came here with a group of friends who are all entrepreneurs and live in various cities and countries around the world.

When we met each other a few years ago, we were only able to meet online, yet they all seemed so familiar to me. It was as though we were long-lost friends who finally reunited.

So we decided to have an official reunion in-person so we could spend time together, work on creative projects, brainstorm and mastermind on our businesses, and attend a conference that's dedicated to bringing diverse professionals together to learn from each other and develop businesses that contribute to humanity in a variety of ways. The organization is called Ethical Businesses Building the Future (EBBF).

We chose Ericeira because of the great proximity to the ocean, beautiful small gardens, and located close to a number of other beautiful cities like Lisbon and Sintra. It's wonderful to be among true friends who remind you of what you're capable of and encourage you to trust your dreams, trust your voice, and trust your path of service in the world.

NICKNAME FOR THIS LEADERSHIP STYLE: EXPLORERS AND DOT CONNECTORS

These amazing leaders around the world have a desire to discover new ways of exploring, understanding, and implementing knowledge. They look deep into the roots of what's happening to engage with a profound feeling of trust as they search for Truth.

They use creative ways to express, explain, and expand on the knowledge they discover and practice.

This is why I affectionately called them the Explorers and Dot-Connectors

DEDICATED TO

Shifu

CORE BELIEFS, VALUES, VANTAGE POINTS, QUALITIES OF THIS LEADERSHIP TEAM

In the service-driven leadership framework, another less common style is Trust and Truth. These leaders are fierce learners and explorers, constantly seeking connections between truth, trust and love.
Individuals who embody this leadership style share their Vantage Points and Values:

- They have an innate desire to seek truth and make meaningful connections between different areas of knowledge.

- They demonstrate a large amount of patience while discovering new ways of seeing things or finding solutions that have become daunting.

- They care deeply about deepening bonds and connections of trust between people, informations, processes, strategies, and goals.

- They seek out ways to develop their skills and can naturally help people to develop their talents and understanding.

- They dive into information to discover new ways of explaining, categorizing, or presenting insights to others - often enjoying bridging gaps of understanding and creating experiences that help people gain clarity and reduce overwhelm.

- They tend to find many ways to say or explain the same thing so that the entire group can be clear and united.

- They often show up trusting themselves and having confidence that doesn't undermine or harm other people's self-confidence; they enjoy supporting or boosting people's confidence.

- They are life-long learners and tend to be interested in discovering how different subjects relate to each other or overlap - which lead to the development of people's understanding and skills.

- People often seek them out to ask for advice, insights, or counsel.

- They don't just tell people what to do or that things are possible. Instead, they help create or redesign practical processes that show people how to trust themselves, even when variables have changed and some things may seem different.

- They promote the belief that deepening knowledge and wisdom is an exciting adventure that should be explored and expanded. They serve as the wind to the sails of the "learning ship".

- These leaders focus their attention on discovering how to connect the dots and brings important details together in order to have greater understanding about how to move forward and make decisions in a discerning, thoughtful way.

There are ways to adapt that don't get people stuck in indecision, while remaining connected to their goals and values, such as integrity, honesty, generosity, consideration, courage, communication, compassion, and creativity.

This is how these leaders show up and contribute to their community or company.

CONTRIBUTIONS TO COMMUNITIES AND CULTURES

Having this Leadership Style of Trust and Truth is a great benefit to any team, community, campus, organization, and company.

They serve as reminders of how important it is to seek opportunities outside of our comfort zones that promote a deeper understanding of knowledge and wisdom that help individuals and the collective. These leaders can also develop and embody a great capacity for patience throughout the learning process, which can help resolve or prevent frustration, disappointment and overwhelm when challenges occur.

'Every soul is here to discover truth.' This quote emphasizes the commitment of individuals embodying this leadership style to continuously seek truth in their own lives. They strive to be lifelong learners, approach learning with humility and enthusiasm, and apply their knowledge and experiences to connect the dots of awareness and understanding.

These leaders aim to inspire others to find how truth and love can be connected, reminding people that the pursuit of truth and its implementation are an act of love.

Another quote that captures the essence of this leadership style is by 'Abdu'l-Bahá: *'When there is love, nothing is too much effort, and there is always time.'*

This quote beautifully conveys the idea that learning and discovering truth is a process requiring patience. It acknowledges that acquiring knowledge and wisdom is not an instantaneous event but rather a gradual and organic journey. It encourages us to extend patience towards ourselves and others as we learn.

In addition, it is crucial for leaders to practice patience with others, especially when they are active participants in their skill development, growth, and knowledge. The more leaders are able to incorporate steps that foster a positive, trust-filled work environment, it creates a magnetic culture that attracts new talent while also retaining the experienced, more seasoned team members.

A HERO'S STORY

A few months after finishing my graduate degree, I made the decision to move to China for two years and work as a physical therapist right after graduating.

Despite not being Chinese and not knowing how to speak Mandarin at the time, I was able to utilize my degree and skills gained in graduate school and clinical internships.

Due to the same physical anatomy and movement of children in Philadelphia, United States and Zhenjiang, China, I could help treat toddlers and young children in China just as I did in Philadelphia.

Although there were changes in language, environment, and culture, many important aspects remained constant.

Both experiences gave me the opportunity to work with colleagues who deeply care about the health and well-being of children, who enjoy collaborating in an inter-disciplinary team to support the goals of each child, and are dedicated to giving the best possible quality of care to all the young people we served.

This decision to step outside my comfort zone while staying connected to my values was one of the most rewarding experiences of my 20s and I still carry these lessons, my incredible mentor, dear friends, and memories very close to my heart.

Meeting my great mentor in China - who was 92 years old when I was introduced to him - was one of the biggest unexpected blessings I could have imagined.

He showed me what patience in the pursuit of excellence looks like. He became my doctor and being looked after by him felt like I had a protective wing surrounding me and I had absolute trust that everything he taught me was both aligned with my values and that they would lead to great results.

Dr. An was a consistent force for generosity and healing - especially in terms of helping people learn how to trust themselves in challenging circumstances - and I learned a great deal every single interaction.

Although he was 92 years old, he looked and moved like he was still in his 50's - teaching kung fu to young adults, training new retirees Tai Chi in the mornings, and mentoring young physicians to have great scientific and kind-hearted approach to helping their patients heal.

Dr. An was a living example of someone who stayed humble and also completely trusted himself as he led his life of service. "Everyone is my teacher," I remember him saying. Initially, I thought he was just saying that to be nice, and then I quickly realized that every word he said was sincere.

He listened to every patient, as though they were able to explain hidden details that were of the utmost importance in finding the correct diagnosis and having a successful treatment outcome.

He asked questions of his students who were decades younger and completely green and inexperienced - like me. His curiosity was unmatched.
I had never met someone with so much wisdom and humility and joy.

He taught me about how to better take care of my heart so that my condition could heal and I'd enjoy a longer life.

He taught me how to ask "better questions" so that I would keep my thoughts focused on my goal and avoid a lot of needless self-sabotage.
He taught me that I was completely invited to be in his company, among his students, among his team of trained doctors, and learn techniques to be a healthier, happier clinician.

Towards the end of my time in China, he gave me an invitation that changed my life and was truly transformational.
I was invited to participate in his team's annual pilgrimage trip across the country to Yunnan and Tibet.
This trip was designed to prepare mentally, physically, and emotionally for the new year and leave all the stress, strain, and pain from the previous year.

At the time, I was so honored to be included since this was a trip only for the team of Chinese doctors, and no foreigner had ever been invited before.

They welcomed me as *"mei-mei"* - which means "little sister" in Mandarin - and said that there's a train ticket for me.

I was so excited because I had secretly longed to go to Tibet and see the western part of China, but thought it would be too difficult to figure out the journey by myself.

Lo and behold, I just had to be patient and because these wonderful friends and mentors trusted me, the path was already getting prepared. I just had to show up and be myself.

Over one month of the journey together was infused with insightful conversations, hot spring treatments, unexpected adventures on the mountain in a snow storm, necessary treatment adjustments to help me prevent altitude sickness, incredible views, making snow angels on top of mountain peaks, monasteries and meditations, hiking and riding horses up exquisite mountains, playing games to strengthen our imagination, trying to record funny and deep moments in my journal, learning some "trash talking" phrases while playing cards, and learning more about how to properly care for my heart.

It took a long time to continuously practice Dr. An's advice, and he created this trip as an opportunity to help each member of his team and his mentees to trust themselves in a variety of unexpected situations. While we each had our own lessons to anchor into our systems and trust ourselves more, we also had so many experiences to build stronger bonds of trust among each other.
No matter what, we all worked together and took care of each other.

IMPACT & INSIGHTS

Dr. An told me that I was meant to have this trip before my contract concluded and it was time for me to return to the United States.
He said that my heart could remain healthy and strong after the treatment, as long as I continue to practice what he taught me and keep trusting the process.

This is why Dr. An was referred to as *"Shifu"* - which means someone who has mastered a skill or expertise. His example of mastery inspired all of us to continue learning and refining our understanding. *Shifu* also reminded me to embrace the new and unfamiliar elements of my new surroundings, and to see them as an opportunity to train and trust my senses. In the two years that I was fortunate enough to learn from him, I realized the deeper value of travel, learning about different cultures by spending quality time with respected mentors and friends, and getting to appreciate their beauty.

As most people who know me could tell you, there isn't a significant moment or a week that goes by that I don't think about *Shifu*, talk about him, or remember the many gems of wisdom he generously shared with me.

Thank you for the opportunity to share the story of *Shifu* with you, dear Reader.

I'll always love and revere him with my whole heart.

SOME WELL-KNOWN PEOPLE WHO REPRESENT THIS LEADERSHIP STYLE

"The purpose of education is to create in a person the ability to look at the world for himself, to make his own decisions…"
James Baldwin

"A life truly lived constantly burns away veils of illusion, burns away what is no longer relevant, gradually reveals our essence, until, at last, we are strong enough to stand in our naked truth."
Marion Woodman

"To make the right choices in life, you have to get in touch with your soul. To do this, you need to experience solitude, which most people are afraid of, because in the silence you hear the truth and know the solutions.
"When you expand your awareness, seemingly random events will be seen to fit into a larger purpose.
"I am here to serve. I am here to inspire. I am here to love. I am here to live my truth.
"Even when you think you have your life all mapped out, things happen that shape your destiny in ways you might never have imagined.
"Love is the ultimate truth at the heart of the universe and transcends all boundaries.
"When you express your unique talents and use them in the service to humanity, you create abundance in your life and in the lives of others."
Deepak Chopra

A NUTRIENT THAT MIRRORS QUALITIES
OF THIS LEADERSHIP STYLE

The way this Leadership Style contributes to healthier communities and a stronger culture reminds me of the way Vitamin C influences the human body.

Vitamin C is a marker for healthy systems in the body, including cardiovascular (heart and blood vessels) and immune system (that helps prevent and fight infections and disease). This nutrient also helps our eyes to function well, helps wounds to heal, and can prevent serious conditions like strokes and cancer.

The protective mechanism of Vitamin C reminds me that there is so much more power in being proactive in our health and prevent problems, as much as possible. The more we can create a healthy ecosystem and systems in the body, the easier it is for our skin, eyes, heart, blood vessels, bones, cartilage, and immune cells to be safeguarded from harmful agents, called free radicals that compromise the healthy tissues.

Having a vibrant culture that values, promotes, supports, safeguards, and encourages truthfulness and trustworthy behaviors acts as a powerful shield against stress points and challenges that chip away at the bonds between people that allow a team, organization, or community to thrive.

REFLECTION QUESTIONS TO PRACTICE
THIS LEADERSHIP QUALITY

Journal or reflect for a few minutes on the following questions to prime your lens of trust-building:

1. **When was there a moment or situation that I trusted myself? (trusted that I was capable, valuable, smart, talented, etc.)**

2. **What could help me - in this moment - to trust myself more, to trust that I have gems, qualities, values within me?**

TREASURE HUNT INVITATION TO TAKE
INSPIRED ACTION

Your invitation:

1. **Think of a person who activates a feeling of trust.**
   Is it something they do?
   Is it something they say?
   Is it something they help other do?

2. **Reach out to someone who leads their life spreading more trust and love with their words and actions, and express your appreciation for how they show up for people.**
   It can be a text, a voice note, a card, a gift, a home visit, a video chat, or any other way that makes you feel happy.
   The important thing is to recognize them and let them know that it matters to you.

10

THE LEADERSHIP STYLE OF INNOVATION & CREATIVITY

Don't ever make decisions based on fear.
Make decisions based on hope and possibility.
Make decisions based on what should
happen, not what shouldn't.
Michelle Obama

A SPECIAL PLACE IN THE WORLD THAT INSPIRED THIS CHAPTER

I started writing this chapter at a cafe at the top of Mount Carmel in Haifa. I was sitting with my brother back in May of 2011, and we found this beautiful spot to get some tea and dessert.
There was an incredible view of the terraces with immaculate gardens on each level. It's one of the places that always gives me a sense of peacefulness.

It also was the first time that my brother and I got to travel internationally, which led to meeting some wonderful new people and life-defining experiences.

NICKNAME FOR THIS LEADERSHIP STYLE: VISIONARIES

Without a shadow of doubt, this Leadership Style group around the world consistently and with great capacity tune into a creative, innovative way of seeing the current reality.

They see what's currently happening and then zoom out to see what could be possible if the current obstacles were to no longer restrict or resist progress or goals from being achieved.

They offer a panoramic vantage point to see the potential reality that could be created, and tap into the feeling of that new reality already existing.

This is why I have called this Leadership Style group of individuals:
The Visionaries.

DEDICATED TO

Alicia

BELIEFS, VALUES, VANTAGE POINTS, AND UNIQUE
QUALITIES OF THIS LEADERSHIP TEAM

The Vantage Points and Values of this Leadership Style:

- They aim to look at the big picture possibilities and see the inherent potential that has yet to be realized

- They notice obstacles along the path to the finish line of the goal, but aren't frustrated or fazed by them

- They believe that there are always alternative pathways that surpass, circumvent, or utilize the challenges or obstacles

- They often see the challenge merely as speed bumps on the path to progress. If others see a wall, they see it as a potential stepping stone that can be used for leverage towards advancement

- They recognize that every challenge is an opportunity for growth and don't get disturbed if new challenges show up.

- They assume every challenge has a solution to take care of it

- They look for many possibilities to bring about meaningful change and progress

- They are fueled by hope and instill this quality into their language

- They don't wait for all the details to be figured out. They like to start as soon as the goal is visualized and the first steps are clarified

- They have a strong belief in humanity's capacity to accomplish remarkable and unprecedented feats.

- They tend to inspire others by emphasizing the power of collaboration and the pursuit of excellence.

- They are "doers" who actively engage in the field of service and gain momentum when they're in movement.

- When they encounter something they value and believe in, they take immediate action, not waiting for everything to be calculated perfectly before action is taken.

- They function as catalysts, utilizing available resources and generating momentum along the way.

- Their goal is to take inspired action and demonstrate that progress is possible

- Their motto revolves around the belief that improvement is always within reach.

- They believe that even small, meaningful changes can create a ripple effect of positive transformation.

CONTRIBUTIONS TO COMMUNITIES AND CULTURES

Developing people who have this Leadership Style contributes to the overall sense of hope, possibilities, and potential into the community and culture.

As these leaders gain capacity, they embody the belief that people can do great things with each other and for each other. This element in the culture is greatly contagious and begins to create ripple effects of thinking outside-the-box and seeing new potential solutions to challenging problems.

Hope and creativity go hand-in-hand and encourages people to believe in the big, bright, beautiful goals.

Instead of getting frustrated or overwhelmed, more people begin to believe that progress can happen, especially when everyone is working together and collaborating well.

Having leaders that embody hope in their words, actions, and systems creates a magnetic culture that promotes a more positive outlook, the bandwidth to dive into creative solutions, and teamwork that can result in more positive changes, progress, and creating the reality that we truly want and need.

Imagine what would be possible when there are more people leading their lives anchored in these qualities, capacities, and perspectives - helping to prevent the flame of hope from burning out and to keep it burning strong and bright.

A HERO'S STORY

When I was 27 years old, I was so incredible satisfied with my work, the clients I took care of, and the team I collaborated with. I was working for a company that I was proud to be part of, and I felt so aligned with the values of the institute and the owners.

It was a values-driven company and the owners cared deeply about serving our clients and community with excellence.

That's when I met "Alicia", who was a high-ranking military officer and part of a special international diplomacy program. Needless to say, from our initial conversation, I felt a bit intimidated by her, her level of experience, her international work, and her overall sense of positivity. It was all very impressive to me and the rest of my team.

After working together for a couple of months, she asked if we could have a private conversation away from everyone else. I assumed something had happened that needed my immediate attention because she and I always spoke freely in the main room where other people were working. In my mind, I was hoping she wasn't upset or frustrated about our work together. However, just to be prepared for the worst-case scenario, I tried to collect myself so I could respond well to any of her complaints.

When we walked into a private consultation room, she smiled and asked how I was doing.

Confused but relieved, I said that I was good and wanted to see how I could help her. In anticipation for her expression to change or for her to share some bad news, I took a deep breath.

To my surprise, she started complimenting me and my professionalism, and how some of the other officers were talking about how much I helped them.

The more she said, the more confused I became because I kept waiting for a problem to be stated.
After a while, she told me that she thinks I could have great success as a consultant that works with leaders who want to make a bigger difference and train more leaders who care about people.

She continued telling me about her vision for the trajectory of my professional path of service, and I was so shocked and trying to catch up to what she was telling me.
She described every step with such detail and clarity, it started to feel like it was actually possible - and I believed that she was seeing something that I couldn't quite see clearly yet, but it felt intriguing.

IMPACT & INSIGHTS

I didn't have any details of how to start creating this new professional reality, but Alicia gave me a clear panoramic view of what I could be doing at some point in the future. It felt expansive and excited - and then a bit scary and unfamiliar when I focused on all the things I didn't know yet.

I never thought of working for myself and having my own consulting business.
I never imagined having clients work with me and refer their friends and colleagues.
I never felt that I could be an entrepreneur - let alone a successful one.

However, Alicia didn't budge nor did she listen to all my reasons for why it couldn't happen.
She continued telling me about what she saw in terms of possibility and potential, and she gave me hope that I would be able to figure out the details and that "life has an interesting way of showing us how to move around the obstacles".

That phrase stayed with me for the rest of that day, and has continued to stay with me for over 15 years.

Alicia helped plant seeds of fresh ideas that needed time and experience to germinate, yet they were always present.

She showed me that it's ok to think of new ways of doing things, even if they are bigger than we think we're ready for.

To practice seeing a goal through the lens of possibility and hope can create a new sense of imagination and creativity.

This is a great way to set ourselves up to reach new goals and realize that we can make our lives feel more expansive and dynamic.

Thank you, Alicia, for showing me how to look at life through a more telescopic, panoramic perspective and vantage point.
That's where new possibilities have the chance to be seen, felt, and then acted on so that they can be created and come into reality.

SOME WELL-KNOWN PEOPLE WHO REPRESENT THIS LEADERSHIP STYLE

"We must accept finite disappointment, but never lose infinite hope."
Martin Luther King Jr.

"Hope is being able to see that there is light despite all the darkness."
Desmond Tutu

"Hope is bravery. The new dawn blooms as we free it. For there is always light if only we're brave enough to see it, if only we're brave enough to be it."
National Youth Poet Laureate, Amanda Gorman

"We have to have leaders who talk to us about hope and the possibility of change, which is what hope is."
Stephen Colbert

A NUTRIENT THAT MIRRORS QUALITIES OF THIS LEADERSHIP STYLE

This Leadership Style shows up in the world much like Vitamin A helps the human body.

Like most nutrients, Vitamin A can help with a variety of physiological systems, such as supporting a healthy immune system, helping babies develop well in the womb, maintain healthy bones and prevent bone fractures.

One of the remarkable things I found about Vitamin A is the way that it helps our eyes.

It is an essential nutrient required for normal vision, preserving our eyesight, and preventing night blindness and age-related decline of vision.

When vision is clear and can stay focused on the goal, the target, or the finish line far in the distance, that adds a powerful element to any community, company, project, or organization.

This Leadership Style of Innovation and Creativity serve like Vitamin A because these leaders can offer the determination to maintain a clear view of the possibilities that are yet to be achieved or created. They serve like the eyes that stay in focus and see what's ahead.

REFLECTION QUESTIONS TO PRACTICE
THIS LEADERSHIP QUALITY

Journal or reflect on the following questions in order to tune your visionary lens:

1. **When have you wanted something that you didn't yet achieve, but you believed it was possible?**

2. **Once you made progress, how did it feel to make progress and see yourself getting closer to the goal that you wanted?**

TREASURE HUNT INVITATION TO TAKE
INSPIRED ACTION

Your Invitation, Dear Reader:

1. **Reflect on someone whose words and actions inspire you to feel hope and new possibilities.**
   A. Look for a person who has made a positive impact, no matter how small, through thinking outside the box or looking at something with a fresh, creative perspective.
   B. Why are these qualities valuable for everyone?

2. **Decide on something you can do to ignite or restore hope in another person.**
   For example: share an uplifting story about a real-life hero or help someone who could use a boost of joy or hope.
   A. Take one inspired action that inspires hope in those who may feel down, low, or despondent.

** Remember, your actions can be given at any time and on any scale that feels right for you.*
** Offer it with kindness and hope that humanity can do bright, beautiful things for each other and with each other.*
B. After taking action, notice how you feel about the experience.

How was the interaction?

Is there anything you would adjust or do differently?

Is there anything you would do again to make the experience more joyful or fulfilling?

11

THE LEADERSHIP STYLE OF EMPOWERMENT & INCLUSION

If there is light in the soul,
There will be beauty in the person.
If there is beauty in the person,
There will be harmony in the house.
If there is harmony in the house,
There will be order in the nation.
If there is order in the nation,
There will be peace in the world.
Chinese Proverb

A SPECIAL PLACE IN THE WORLD THAT INSPIRED THIS CHAPTER

A cafe outside of Sintra, Portugal that has the best freshly squeezed orange juice - oranges from the southern part of Portugal called Algarve. There's a very relaxed vibe with a very friendly staff that easily flow from one language to another - depending on the accent of the clients sitting at their tables. In the course of 20 minutes, I hear people speaking Portuguese, English, Spanish, French, German, Dutch, and Italian.

Every table of patrons seem comfortable, at home, welcomed, and able to enjoy the beautiful view of the sunbeams dancing on the waves of the Atlantic Ocean, rhythmically touching on the beach in front of the cafe.

NICKNAME FOR THIS LEADERSHIP STYLE: INVITATION MAKERS

After meeting and working with hundreds of people who embody this Leadership Style, I noticed a consistent trait that they all have in common. They create a welcoming, inviting, warm environment around them so that people feel safe around them. They also tend to thoughtfully design experiences to activate a feeling of belonging for all the people present.

This is why I've given them the nickname: **Invitation-Makers**.

DEDICATED TO

Dr. Amir

BELIEFS, VALUES, VANTAGE POINTS, AND UNIQUE QUALITIES OF THIS LEADERSHIP TEAM

The Vantage Point and Values of this Leadership Style:

- They are acutely aware when people aren't feeling seen, valued, invited, welcomed, respected, and included.

- They have a deep desire for people (themselves included) to experience a true sense of empowerment and encouragement to be seen for who they truly are and share their skills.

- They see the innate value of human beings and realize that we are stronger, more resilient, and more capable when we feel connected to others and they feel connected to us.

- They want everyone to believe that they have worth that goes beyond their physical appearance, their material possessions, their backgrounds, their family status, their level of education, where they live, and their age.

- They dare to see all people as worthy of respect, justice, and opportunities to live a fulfilling life.

- They seek out ways to help people feel included and welcomed, regardless of their differences or similarities.

- They enjoy creating a culture around them that transcends barriers and patterns of exclusion or separations between people.

- They create opportunities that brings people from various backgrounds together for a shared goal, vision, and values.

- They design experiences that enable people to show up with their uniqueness and distinct diversity and feel a sense of belonging.

- They give people permission to have a place to belong - and remember that they have value, merit, and worthiness .

- They light up when groups of people are encouraged to be present and feel safe in their environment with each other.

CONTRIBUTIONS TO COMMUNITIES AND CULTURES

What sets these leaders apart is a core belief deeply ingrained in their character from a young age. Throughout their lives, they have displayed a keen sensitivity to others' feelings of inclusion or exclusion. Witnessing people experience a sense of belonging and connection brings them immense joy. Conversely, when they witness disconnection or exclusion, it compels them to take action.

To them, the power of unity and inclusion is transformative. When individuals feel connected, supported, and cherished within a group, they exude confidence, and limitless possibilities come to life. These leaders possess an exceptional ability to foster trust swiftly. In their presence, hope blossoms, and a profound sense of trust permeates the atmosphere.

Their approach revolves around seeking common ground, using it as a catalyst for unity.

They recognize that deep down, we all share the desire for merit, worthiness, and a sense of belonging.

They believe in celebrating individual uniqueness while emphasizing our shared needs. People cannot be at their best when they feel abandoned, isolated, or alone in despair.

As human beings, our goal should be to help everyone feel strong and capable. We all require support, and a magical transformation occurs when support becomes a reciprocal process of nurturing. Even the individuals receiving assistance can find ways to give back and support others.

This reciprocity strengthens them, engenders respect, and helps them realize their full potential.

At the heart of this leadership style lies the catalyst: welcoming individuals, embracing inclusivity, and ensuring everyone feels worthy of belonging.

They encourage individuals to express their unique qualities while fostering an environment where all can coexist harmoniously and serve together.

Imagine having people all over the world - and in your own life - who lead their lives with this vantage point and developed capacities to contribute to your community.

A HERO'S STORY

When I was a young professional recently back in the United States from my time working in China, I had the good fortune to know a wonderful ambassador of this Leadership Style of Empowerment & Inclusion. We'll call him Dr. Amir.

He was a tenured professor at a prestigious college, and he knew me from when I was student and very shy about public speaking.

He generously extended an invitation for me to be a guest lecturer for one of his fourth year classes studying Cross-Cultural Psychology. I instantly felt like there was no way that I could do a good enough job and felt like his students would be sheerly disappointed, bored, or both.

I tried to graciously decline, but he insisted that this was something he had been thinking about and felt that I would do a great job with the students. Unfortunately, I couldn't avoid the invitation and reluctantly accepted. He explained his vision for my work and how important it is for me to start training my voice to speak to groups of people.

Dr. Amir's points were so empowering and encouraging, I started to believe him and forgot why I should be nervous. He had convinced me that I was in the right place at the right time and already had plenty of helpful experiences and insights to share with the students.

I followed his lead and became excited and started to look forward to designing my presentation. When I arrived to the college campus, he was there to greet me.

I felt so welcomed. Then he offered to introduce me to some of his colleagues and research assistants. I felt so included. In a matter of 60 minutes, I went from feeling uncertain about my presence on such a respected campus to feeling at ease and like a belonged in their space.

Although I was a visitor and a guest, Dr. Amir designed the experience to help me feel welcomed and truly like there was a place for me to serve the students. He didn't have to convince me with words or logic. Instead, he showed me and welcomed me with the way he led the events of the day.

IMPACT & INSIGHTS

Because of Dr. Amir's encouragement and embodiment of this Leadership Style, I discovered that I really enjoy presenting and speaking to groups of people. Although I still have feel some nervousness leading up to the event, I remember the way Dr. Amir created a reality that showed me how it's ok for me to step into new spaces, with new people, with larger sized organizations.

Regardless of the location, stature, size, or reputation of the institution or organization - I can still belong and find a way to share my service with the people there.

Thanks to Dr. Amir, I've received many invitations and referrals to speak and present my framework to colleges in the United States, as well as to conferences attended by Directors and Officers of the United Nations and the World Health Organization.

It's incredibly humbling and gratifying to be able to share this work with more service-driven people all over the world.

There's something very special about the power of an invitation given through thoughtful empowerment and encouragement. Dr. Amir is masterful at this, and I thank him dearly.

SOME WELL-KNOWN PEOPLE WHO REPRESENT THIS LEADERSHIP STYLE

*"In diversity there is beauty and there is strength.
We all should know that diversity makes for a rich tapestry,
and we must understand that all the threads of the tapestry
are equal in value no matter what their color."*
Maya Angelou.

"Strength lies in differences, not in similarities."
Stephen Covey.

*"We need diversity of thought in the world
to face the new challenges."*
Tim Berners-Lee.

"Learn to enjoy and respect each other's differences."
Fred Meijer.

A NUTRIENT THAT MIRRORS QUALITIES
OF THIS LEADERSHIP STYLE

This Leadership Style serves any team, community, organization, and culture the way Vitamin D serves the human body.

Vitamin D is vital to bone health, muscle movement, nerve connections to the brain, and immune system function. Having enough of this nutrient is important to prevent bone fractures when falls or other injuries occur.

Having enough empowerment and inclusion also makes people, organizations, and communities more resilient to forces that can harm people's sense of worthiness and value, fray connections between people, and weaken confidence and creativity.

REFLECTION QUESTIONS TO PRACTICE
THIS LEADERSHIP QUALITY

Journal or reflect on the following questions to prime your empowerment lens:

1. **Think of a time where you felt welcomed, invited, or a sense of belonging.**
   A. **How did you this experience impact you?**
   B. **Who helped you feel connected or included as a result of their words or actions?**

TREASURE HUNT INVITATION TO TAKE
INSPIRED ACTION

Reflecting on the qualities of Empowerment and Inclusion, think of a person (or group of people) who could feel more connected, welcomed, or included.

This could be someone who is new to the neighborhood, hasn't yet made friends in their environment, or seems to be disconnected or lonely because they are different from the majority of the people around them.

You're invited to brainstorm a way to help this person feel welcomed, included, or invited to participate and join the conversation, join an activity, join in a conversation.

You can start with any action that feels light and right for you.

A small step or invitation is fine.

"What action would lead to the best possible ripple effect for this person to no longer feel separate or alone - but instead to feel more seen with kindness, valued, and included?"

After you take inspired action, reflect on how it went and if it feels like something you'd like to do again - either for the same person or for another person.

Notice the feeling of being in that heroic moment. Allow yourself to fully immerse in the experience of adding something positive and uplifting to someone's day.

It is not our differences that divide us.
It is our inability to recognize, accept,
and celebrate those differences.
Audre Lorde

SUMMARY HIGHLIGHTS

In over two decades of work, I've noticed that some of the most influential, respected, and successful leaders are embodying qualities that are different from the historical template of "leaders".

After thousands of Leadership Style assessments, I'm confident that there's a newer, stronger, more welcomed type of leaders who are not interested in wielding their power to make others weaker, disempowered, or live in more fear and scarcity.

There have been plenty of examples of people who are using this outdated system of using their qualities and resources to do harm, cause more suffering, and divide human beings.

Instead, there's an emerging type of leadership style that care deeply about their own lives and also the lives of all people. They desire a feeling of fulfillment, joy, and impact that improves the quality of life for all people - regardless of where they live, what they look like, and what language they speak.

These leaders are setting a refreshing, recharging, inspiring example of how to live a life fully, thoughtfully, intentionally, wisely, and lovingly. They deeply care about the entire human family and want to encourage the next generations to develop their capacities to do the same.

They feel a sense of connection to the generations who came before them and the generations who come after them, and they act with a devotion to create a world that will be good for our future generations.

All nine Service-Driven Leadership Styles that I have researched, explored, and worked with each contributes to the creation of a more vibrant, unified, and healthier culture. Whether it is within a community, family, or organization, the impact of these nine Leadership Styles ripples outward, extending to the broader society.

The ultimate objective of all nine Leadership Styles is to recognize and nourish the 19+ needs that allow people to be their most whole, true, actualized selves. In this state, people can become more ready, willing, and able to harmoniously contribute to the development of a thriving, interconnected, and abundant culture. Powerful collaboration, innovation, and progress become a natural result of a healthier community and ecosystem.

By fostering such an environment, individuals are empowered to attain better health and balance, deeper awareness of themselves and others, and achieve greater success that feels fulfilling. Ultimately, having more people who choose to lead their lives in a way that increases the level of integrity, impact, and joy in their lives. This is something that we can all feel called to do and proud to be a part of… in our own unique and diverse way.

You're invited to keep practicing, noticing, and diving into your unique Leadership Style.

You're invited to decide to be part of this global community of service-driven leaders who show up each day - perfectly imperfect - but very much on purpose and with a purpose.

You're welcome to have a seat on the stage that this symphony of humanity is playing - in tune with your own instrument so you can play in tune with more instruments.

With each of us playing our part and contributing our unique combination of talents, skills, gifts, and resources, we find a way to lead our lives from a posture of learning, a position of integrity, and a possibility to take action that helps others while also helping you experience a good feeling in your heart.

Consider yourself a musician that's part of the process of creating a symphony.

The musicians are the ones who play the notes and are the first ones to feel the vibrations and beauty of the music.

The music touches the musicians first and then its shared with everyone else in the space.

That is what my experience has shown me over these last two decades.

When people show up to help others, their own qualities become stronger, more defined and refined.

The intention is to enrich the lives of other people, and in the process, their own lives become more meaningful, more fulfilling, and more abundant.

The ripple effects project outwardly to potentially touch the lives of people in your household, community, team, project, company, or organization - and the impact often is reciprocated back in unexpected, helpful, supportive ways.

Hopefully, you're discovering that everyone has the potential to be a leader. Specifically, everyone can be a service-driven leader by making the conscious decision to embody their vision, values, and voice to enhance both their own and others' quality of life.

Once you've made this choice, you are already on the path to becoming a service-driven leader.

By taking action based on this self-identification, you become part of a global team working towards positive change for humanity.

You contribute as a constructive force, utilizing your unique talents and unleashing your creativity to experience satisfaction, fulfillment, and joy.

We have learned that creating an improved culture, community, or country requires diverse leadership styles and perspectives.

Afterall, our differences should not create discord but rather complement one another.

Each of us possesses highly valuable and special qualities that, when harmonized, create space for everyone to contribute their gifts and perspectives. Embracing diversity nourishes both ourselves and others, resulting in a fulfilling and creative way of living.

This discussion encompasses not only leadership styles but also qualities essential for building a thriving culture. It is a culture-building system or toolkit that encourages active participation from as many individuals as possible.

Wherever we find ourselves, we can contribute to a constructive force that enhances the lives of everyone within that ecosystem, including ourselves.

Embrace curiosity about your unique vantage points and leadership qualities, while also valuing and exploring those of others. Your gifts can support others, and theirs can support yours, fostering an abundant-minded way of being.

Finally, I invite you to discover your own unique leadership style. You have gained insight into all nine leadership styles and experienced being an ambassador for each of them.

Now, it's time to delve deeper into your primary leadership style by engaging with the questions provided in the link below. This opportunity will offer invaluable insight into how you can operate with integrity, make a greater impact, and experience even more joy.

In this book, I hope you found some gems and knowledge acquired throughout decades of study, observation, and analysis.

Sharing knowledge is valuable, but the true power lies in applying that knowledge.

It is essential to become aware of our leadership abilities and utilize them to foster growth and build flourishing communities.

As a reader, you can start by studying the book and implementing its principles in your own life.

If you desire guidance and support on this transformative journey, you can book a call with the author to take the first step together towards building a brighter future and becoming part of a remarkable new community with a fresh attitude.

This call marks the beginning of a transformative process that will bring your aspirations to life.

www.leadyourdesign.com/free-leadership-design-call

A MESSAGE OF HOPE AND ENCOURAGEMENT ABOUT LEADERSHIP

We humans have so many unique distinctions, diverse cross-sections, and differences and we also also have so much in common.

It's important to notice the variety of needs that we all require and let that be a reminder of our shared humanity.
The more needs that are met, the more people can exist in peace and live fulfilling lives.

It's also important to realize the multi-faceted ways we are unique and have our own vantage points and lenses to experience life. We all have capacities, potential strengths, and mechanisms for developing our talents.

We all have the same needs, but oftentimes, in different amounts, ratios, and order of priority in which needs are important to tend to first.
We all have blind spots and gaps in our understanding, because we have lived one life with a certain amount of time to learn, grow, and have experiences of our own.

The more we create room to discover more of what we can naturally and intentionally bring to the table - wherever we happen to live, study, work, or travel - we discover ways that our contributions can close the gaps of needs that are around us.

Develop our potential can help others invest in developing their potential, and the expression of our talents and skills can lead to a community that flourishes.

Each person can create new ripples of positive change that allows reciprocal learning and inspiration.

Service-driven leaders help develop more proactive protagonists to the processes that bring about more solutions that help people be their best selves.

A new paradigm and cycle emerges:
When more people can contribute their gifts in collaborative ways → uplifts the quality of life for more people → more safety and sense of security → less stress and less fear → more resources flow to capacity-building → more energy and time for creative solutions → less suffering → more development of human potential.

The cycle continues to grow and become refined with the necessary details for each community or organization.

We don't have to be the same in order to be connected and united. We can show up with our diversity seen and valued, and we can work together with our complimentary strengths → growth and expansion → values are honored → more help is offered → more appreciation and reciprocation → create a thriving culture and community.

There's enough space and opportunities for many cross-sections of diversity to be seen, valued, welcomed, nourished, expressed, and part of the solutions.

The world is dehydrated and ready for more people to shine a light on their gifts and walk on their unique paths of service and contribution.

FINAL THOUGHTS AND YOUR NEXT INVITATION

In this book, we've explored some of the unique elements of how diversity can be a game-changing foundation to any community, company, culture, or organization.

We've gotten to become acquainted with the 9 Service-Driven Leadership Styles in this framework, what they value, and how they can contribute to a more vibrant, thriving culture and successful communities.

You've also gotten to learn about a few real-life heroes who accompanied me during important life moments, and how they each embody outstanding qualities that reflect more respect, more understanding, and more possibilities for a brighter future.

I invite you to have fun with the portions at the end of each chapter so you can put your unique leadership lens into practice. Completing the Reflection Questions and doing the Treasure Hunt activities allow you to appreciate your own leadership qualities, as well as benefit from other people's vantage points.

Practicing showing up and cultivating environments that move away from any competition or criticism is a powerful attribute of many service-driven leaders. They stand for equity and they speak up to support the needs of others. They lead their lives with a focus to improve the quality of life within their sphere of impact.

This activates powerful replacements to criticism and contention with a higher degree of compassion and care, thoughtful communication and understanding, and a deeper awareness of how to create ripples of hope through taking noble action.

Perhaps this moment in human history is significant and timely for as many people as possible to lead their lives with integrity, impact, and joy in order to elevate the quality of life for our collective human family.

I wish you countless confirmations and support as you continue polishing your "gems of inestimable value" for everyone's highest good.

I welcome your thoughts on how this Service-Driven Leadership framework could support you, your colleagues, or industry leaders whom you admire and respect.

To the following questions, you're invited to email your insights and inspirations to: hello@leadyourdesign.com

- What you enjoyed most about this book.

- What story or Treasure Hunt activity impacted you the most.

- Topics or content you would enjoy learning about in future books or events.

- Ask to join the Global Leaders Inner Circle to receive first access to gifts, special experiences, and goodies that we create for our community.

ACKNOWLEDGING ALL THE PEOPLE OF THE LANDS WE LIVE: A BLESSING FOR OUR WORLD

Dear Reader,

Wherever you happen to be reading this book, I hope you are safe and well.

Although I've lived in only 4 countries, I realize that there are countless places that we humans currently live, visit, work, and study.

While I am not part of an Indigenous Nation or Native Tribe, I have friends since childhood who have welcomed me with open hearts and kindness.

My father had also had a very special relationship with the Chippewa Nation - or as they call themselves *Anishinaabeg* - when he was a new student in the United States and was invited as a friend and son.

This meant a lot to my father, as he was away from his entire family and learning about his new country, new culture, and new language.

With an open and respectful heart, I wish to send my sincere appreciation and warmest regards to honor all the ancestors and generations of Indigenous Nations who have cared for the lands around the world where you and I now have the gift of living on. I pay my respect to Elders both past, present, and future.

May every place on earth become healthier, experience more balance, and blossom for everyone's highest good.

May every person in every place feel more at peace, healthier, mindful, and able to feel part of our human family and at home in our world.

Jaleh Zandieh:

Global Leadership Expert | Seeker of Hidden Gems | Tea Lover

Jaleh helps service-driven leaders - from CEO's to U.N. Directors to Grammy-Award winning artists - discover how to create more impact in the world without burning out from the work that lights them up.

They learn proven processes that transform stress into strengths, so they can inspire more people through their example and make their vision for humanity become more of a reality.

Her research-based framework is based on 2 decades of work that helps teams become more inclusive and harmonize the diversity that is represented. Leaders discover how their organizations can better express their values, vantage point, and voice... powerfully, authentically, and sustainably.

Jaleh designs experiences that help entrepreneurs and industry leaders set their teams up for more success by creating a stronger, resilient ecosystem of inclusion and collaboration.

She creates customized trainings that enable each team member to contribute to the goals of the organization aligned with their unique Leadership Style.

This supports each person to be nourished by the nine essential elements of a thriving culture and community.

Jaleh's foundational Philosophy:
"Diversity is meant to nourish and help us flourish."

When she's not creating experiences for innovative leaders around the world, she's filling her passport with stamps to discover hidden gems, savoring exotic teas with loved ones, enjoying live music, and spending time in nature with her husband in Portugal.

How You Can Connect with Jaleh:

1. Complimentary gift Leadership Style results call to discover your unique Leadership Style and Primary Strengths: **https://www.leadyourdesign.com/form**

2. To learn more about Jaleh, her signature trainings, speaking topics, interview guest, and ways she can support your organization or event: **https://www.leadyourdesign.com/**

APPRECIATION, ACKNOWLEDGEMENTS & GRATITUDE LIST

Thank you Mom and Dad for being an example of the power, courage, and resilience a family can have when it's nourished by diversity.

Thank you Ata for growing up with me, for growing strong with me, for growing in service to so many people whose lives are better because of you.

Thank you Alex Joon for being the co-architect of our Fortress of Well-Being, the microphone to my voice, my partner, my Left Wing, the man of my dreams, my "alma gemêa", my Heartmate.

Thank you to my A-Team. I wouldn't be here without you and I wouldn't be me without your unfailing love and support.

Thank you Shifu for helping my heart heal and for saving my life. I'm glad to still be here.

Thank you to my Aunts who shower me with so much love and strength.

Thank you to my Uncles who say fewer words but show up for me and show me what's possible when men and women support each other fully.

Thank you Peixoto family for inviting me into your family and making me feel so welcome so that Portugal can feel like home.

Thank you Linda for being by my side during the post-shooting challenges and being a true friend at a difficult time. The impact of your kindness is still felt.

Thank you to my teacher, Mr. Baker, who showed me how to organize and write stories.

Thank you to my mentors who took me under their wings and guided me, not because they had to, but because they wanted to.

Thank you Selena Soo for embodying the voice, beliefs, and actions of what a next-level community-builder looks like. The people who I've met through you are true gems, and you are the radiant catalyst of these enriching relationships.

Thank you Denise for believing in my framework, my research, my system, my story, my voice, and envisioning what this book could be - before it was close to being a book.

Thank you Jess for your encouragement, generosity, and dedication to make my business a place where people can learn and experience my framework, but also connect to a profound part of themselves. Your talents seem to have no limits.

Thank you to my Global Gals for our inspiring, heart filling group gatherings. You helped me face my fears and step up anyway.

Thank you Sherry for being a fairy Godmother to Liv.

Thank you to all the service-driven leaders who participated in my research, workshops, trainings, consultations, team-building events, CEO retreats, and virtual events.
I wish you all continued success, inspiration, and impact that "brings your heart nothing but joy".

Thank you to all the service-driven leaders-in-training who are ready, willing, and available to contribute your diverse talents, care, and gifts to improve the lives of others.

May you discover paths, doors, and opportunities to experience the joy of service.

www.ingramcontent.com/pod-product-compliance
Lightning Source LLC
Chambersburg PA
CBHW040137160726
48006CB00014B/1520

9 7 9 1 2 8 1 3 8 5 0 1 6